Confessions
of a Prayer
Slacker

by Diane Moody

Charlotte, Tennessee 37036

Library of Congress Control Number: 2010928043

ISBN 978-0-9824832-4-4 (softcover)

Interior design by Marisa Jackson.

10 11 12 13 14 15 16 17 18 19 — 10 9 8 7 6 5 4 3 2 1

Manufactured in the United States of America

To Ken

Have I told you today
how much I love you?

Praise for Diane Moody

"Written to the slacker in all of us, Diane Moody turns our 'tired' into triumph by helping us clear the path to meaningful time with God."
—Nicole Johnson, author and dramatist with Women of Faith

"I've read several books about prayer over the years but this one is by far my favorite! Diane is a gifted writer who will help you uncover so many misconceptions you've picked up which have damaged your prayer life over the years. I can't tell you how many 'ah-ha' moments I had in the midst of this enlightening, inspiring, read. I've been inspired to start an entire new prayer journey!"
—Pete Wilson, pastor of Cross Point Community Church, Nashville, Tennessee, and author of *Plan B*

"With fresh writing and transparent stories, Diane Moody has done more than craft a book. She's shared her heart in a way that I was inspired to seek to know God better, deeper. I have to admit once I started reading *Confessions of a Prayer Slacker*, I couldn't read more than a few pages at a time. Why? My heart was so pricked I had to put down the book and PRAY! Success indeed!"
—Tricia Goyer, author of twenty-four books, including *Blue Like Play Dough: The Shape of Motherhood in the Grip of God*

"For many years, I have watched Diane's passion and commitment to prayer. Forged by fire, God has given her a deep love for prayer which is contagious! This is not your everyday, ho-hum look at prayer. You will find yourself smiling . . . okay, maybe outright belly laughing. But you will also be challenged, motivated and (prayerfully), radically impacted in your relationship with God. *Prayer Slacker* may just kick-start

your conversations with God in a way no tall latte ever could!"
—Teresa Nardozzi, Director of Women's Ministries
at First Baptist Church of Indian Rocks at Largo, Florida

"*Confessions of a Prayer Slacker* is phenomenal. It offers a new perspective on prayer in such a straightforward, genuine, and visual way. It grabbed and kept my attention from start to finish, through both laughter and tears. You have inspired me to stop being a slacker and start praying. Thank you for making it personal."
—Cathy Weisbrodt, Nashville, Tennessee

"As a homeschooling mother of four, it is very easy for me to have a litany of excuses not to have a regular, daily prayer time with God. Diane Moody's book has greatly encouraged me to meet with God daily and remember that prayer is a very meaningful way of developing a deep, committed, awesome relation with my Maker."
—Anne Connell, Tallahassee, Florida

"Diane's style is easy to read and honest. Prayer slackers beware! This book will grip your heart and challenge you to go to the next level."
—Dennis Hayford, Director, Greater Mobile Area
Fellowship of Christian Athletes, Mobile, Alabama

"In *Confessions of a Prayer Slacker,* Diane Moody's fast-paced, witty, and at times painfully honest writing vividly illustrates that having a 'prayer life' is much more than just another Christian habit or spiritual cliché. It can be a joyful and meaningful way to change your life, and those around you, forever."
—Randy Elrod, author of *Sex, Lies & Religion*

Table of Contents

Introduction

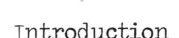

How long will you stay in bed, you slacker?
When will you get up from your sleep?
—Proverbs 6:9, HCSB

The mere fact that you picked up a book about prayer tells me you're probably a Christian. You believe Jesus is the Son of God; and somewhere along the line, you asked Jesus to come into your heart, meaning you have a relationship with Him. Maybe you grew up in church, following the Lord from an early age. Maybe you were one of thousands at a Billy Graham crusade who went forward when the invitation was given, making a commitment to follow Christ for the rest of your life. Maybe you read a book by Rick Warren and learned about a purpose for your life through Jesus, or one of Max Lucado's books that gave you a vivid, more personal vision of Christ's gift of eternal life. Maybe the words of a hymn struck a chord in your heart. Maybe you became interested in Christ after observing a friend or neighbor who year after year exemplified the love of Christ in everything he ever did.

Or maybe yours was a most unusual moment of truth. Like twentieth-century American writer and editor Whittaker Chambers. A former member of the

1

Communist party and a Soviet spy, Chambers tells of his conversion in his autobiography.

> My daughter was in her high chair. I was watching her eat. She was the most miraculous thing that had ever happened in my life. My eye came to rest on the delicate convolutions of her ear—those intricate, perfect ears . . . The thought passed through my mind: 'No, those ears were not created by any chance coming together of atoms in nature (the Communist view). They could have been created only by immense design.' . . . I did not know that, at that moment, the finger of God was first laid upon my forehead.[1]

Whoa. I get chills every time I read that. To think that the Creator of the universe, knowing exactly how Chambers' mind worked, would draw his eye to notice the intricacies of his baby's ear, and from that moment—that split-second of understanding—would help him come to believe in God. Talk about amazing grace!

Millions of people have been drawn to the Lord throughout history, each arriving at their belief on their own unique path. Sometimes we arrive there at the end of a broken dream or the result of some life-changing, crushing tragedy. We find ourselves without hope or purpose—apart from Him. Others simply acknowledge there's got to be something more to life than mere human existence.

Each of us has an exclusive story telling how we came to find God. For centuries, preachers have told us about the "God-shaped hole" in all of us, put there by a loving Creator who wants to have a personal relationship with each one of us. How we respond to that holy hole in us makes all the difference.

Call me crazy, but every time I hear of another acclaimed "apparition" of Jesus or the Virgin Mary, I'm reminded just what a vacuum that God-shaped hole has come to be in our culture. When we lived near Clearwater, Florida, in December of 1996, one such apparition appeared on the side of a bank building on busy Highway 19. Just google "Marian Apparition in Clearwater" to see what all the fuss was about. Granted, I'm usually rather skeptical of these things, but I must say the resemblance was striking. The 60-foot image, apparently caused by a residue from sprinklers that routinely splashed against the two-story glass windows, became such a popular shrine for thousands of travelers from around the world that the bank inside had to close. Gridlock traffic required constant police presence. Then in 2004 an angry teenager threw a rock through the glass, shattering the image.

Of course, Clearwater wasn't the first host of such religious apparitions. Back in 1978, a New Mexico woman noticed the mournful face of Jesus in skillet markings on her tortilla. More than 8,000 people journeyed to her home to view the image. Over 8,000! Then in 2004, a grilled cheese sandwich with the image of the Virgin Mary ended up selling on eBay for $24,000. Gee, for that kind of money, maybe I should check out the moldy items in my refrigerator. Yes, even now I see it—there, in Monday's meatloaf. It's the baby Jesus in a manger. Quick! Someone call Geraldo Rivera! This is *huge*!

Okay, maybe I got carried away. And if these bizarre renderings somehow bring even one life to a saving faith in Christ, then I take back my sarcastic ridicule. But seriously, what could possibly drive tens of thousands to search for Jesus in a burrito or Mary in some holy toast?

I believe it's that same God-shaped vacuum that dwells inside each of us. We know there's something there, tugging at our souls. But we're so out of touch with our Creator that we don't even know what that "tug" is all about or where it's coming from. So we look everywhere else on the planet to fill the void. With money, with material possessions, with relationships, with drugs and alcohol . . . It's as if we're on a mission to fill the void with everything *but* Him. Still, He never gives up. He keeps tugging and tugging and tugging. Why? Because God longs to have a personal relationship with you!

It doesn't get any more personal than that. He loves you. And He wants to spend time with you.

And that's where prayer comes in. If daily prayer has not been a part of your life as a believer, I can't wait for you to discover what's in store for you. I can tell you this: when you start spending time alone with God every day, you will never be the same. Friend, that's a money-back guarantee.

But if you've not had that "come to Jesus" encounter in your life, I want you to take a moment and flip over to page 161, to a section called "How to Become a Christian." There you'll find an explanation of what it means to follow Christ, then a simple prayer that will give you a chance to take care of the most important business in your life.

Finally, one more note before we begin. I feel the need to come clean, so let me just put it out there in bold print.

OFFICIAL AUTHOR DISCLAIMER:
I am not an authority on prayer.

I am *not* a preacher, priest, rabbi, minister, nun, evangelist, or seminary professor, nor am I a theologian with a boatload of credentials. Actually, I did earn a Ph.T. diploma—"Putting Hubby Through"—from a seminary in Texas, but that was more about paying the bills than studying the tenets of faith. Oh, I typed plenty of term papers for said husband on subjects such as systematic theology, apologetics, bibliology, hermeneutics, eschatology, and a bunch of other terms that all sound Greek to me.

Don't get me wrong. I spent plenty of time praying during those early years in our marriage:

- God, please help us be able to pay the rent this month.
- Lord, please help me endure this stupid job until Ken graduates.
- Father, why on earth did you make Texas so darn HOT?!
- And what's with all the big hair around here? These women look like a bunch of Texas tumbleweeds!

But unless typing and prayer-whining qualify me as some kind of prayer guru, then you'd have to agree that I'm no expert on the subject. In other words, if you're looking for teachings from one of the All-Stars of Christianity, I'm not your girl. What I can offer is an entire lifetime of struggling when it comes to prayer.

I've got shelves lined with books about prayer. I've tried prayer formulas. I even tried "praying the scriptures" when that technique appeared on the Christian horizon. Sometimes I'd be inspired by a sermon on the subject and recommit myself to pray daily. I'd buy a new notebook to organize my praying. I'd pick a time of day that best suited my schedule. And off I'd go ... for a day or two. Time after time, I'd make the effort only to fail again and again. And with each failure, I'd hear that sarcastic and belittling voice in my head reminding me once again what a loser I was and what a sorry excuse for a Christian I'd become.

And so it was, year after year, decade after decade, I accumulated a mountain of self-imposed guilt. Eventually I gave up, convinced I'd never have a faithful and meaningful prayer life. And for someone who's been in church since before I was born (Mom never missed a Sunday), that is not a good place to be.

Still, I know I'm not alone in this on-again, off-again battle. Show of hands: how many of you can say your prayer life is a consistent, daily habit, rich and full and spiritually satisfying? Wait. Maybe I should ask it another way. When was the last time you had a genuine, heart-to-heart chat with God? For the record, praying for a winning lottery ticket or a parking space close to the mall does not count.

Come on, be honest. Do you pray? I mean *really* pray. That shut-out-the-world, one-one-one, totally-focused, praising, worshiping, talking, and listening kind of prayerful communication with your heavenly Father, who loves you and yearns to spend time with you?

Right about here, you'd be duly impressed if I tossed in a few statistics about how many people pray, how often they pray, and how prayer has affected their lives. There are plenty of studies out there, all reaching conflicting conclusions depending on who is asking the questions, how they ask those questions, and what their underlying agenda is. But in the end, none of that really matters. Because my heart's desire for this book is about *your* prayer life. Helping *you* find out what's standing in the way of spending quality time every single day with God—the God who made you and cares enough about you to count the number of hairs on your head, for crying out loud! How precious is that?!

So once and for all, let's take a hard look at this matter of prayer. Don't worry. I won't be bombarding you with buckets of Latin or Greek terms (just a couple), nor will I be doing an exegesis of scripture. (Is it just me, or does "exegesis" sound like Exit, Jesus? And I'm sorry, but that's just wrong.) Instead, let's see if we can't drop-kick all the excuses and find out about the significant, intimate treasure that awaits each one of us if only we'll make time to spend with God.

Chapter 1

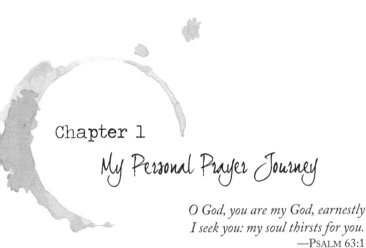

My Personal Prayer Journey

O God, you are my God, earnestly
I seek you: my soul thirsts for you.
—Psalm 63:1

Okay, Okay. I know I said this book is about you, but first I need to give you a little background about my own experience. Why? Because you need to know I've really struggled to learn these life lessons. I'm guessing you've had similar struggles if you've ever tried to be even remotely faithful in your prayer life. And if you're new to the whole concept of prayer, I hope you'll discover at least a glimmer of inspiration to start making prayer as much a part of your every day life as breathing, starting today.

The first time I learned about having a personal prayer life happened on my first trip to church camp. I think I was in the fourth grade, so I must have been around nine or ten years old. Nunny Cha-Ha was a Southern Baptist summer camp for girls in Oklahoma. If you and I were having this discussion face to face, at this point I would break into song, serenading you with the Nunny Cha Ha camp song. After nearly half a century, I still remember that goofy little jingle. I'll spare us both the embarrassment and move along.

The focus of that week was "learning how to listen to the voice of God" in what was dubbed "My Quiet Time with God." You have to admire the camp leaders' intent, but let's be honest. Most pre-adolescents are clueless about such deeply spiritual goals, let alone the discipline to follow through on a daily basis. Still, good little camperettes that we were, we trekked across the campground after our counselors told us to find our "special place" to meet with God each day.

My special place was beneath a big tree. Like the infamous land-run settlers of Oklahoma's colorful history, I staked out the perfect location. I busily cleared the dirt beneath my tree and lined it with little rocks, fashioned a cross out of two twigs, stuck it in the ground near the tree, and declared that it was good. I wiped my hands on my madras Bermudas, then plopped down, cross-legged on the dirt, ready to meet God. For an hour. One *very long* hour. Just me and God. God and me. Every single day of camp. Did I mention these quiet times were supposed to last an entire hour? I tried. Really I did.

"Now I lay me down to sleep . . . "

No. Wait. That's a prayer for babies. I can surely do better than that. Ah! I've got it! The Lord's Prayer! Much more grown-up. So I closed my eyes and recited the familiar words.

"Our Father, Who art in heaven . . . "

Art? I like art. I hope we get to paint this week. Maybe some watercolor . . .

"Hallowed be Thy name."

I've never liked my name. Diane. It's just so plain. Why couldn't Mom and Dad have named me Veronica? Or

Tabitha? Or Maria—like Maria Von Trapp in *The Sound of Music*. Oh my gosh, I love that movie!

"Thy kingdom come, Thy will be done . . . "

Be done, be done, be done . . . will this Quiet Time ever BE DONE? I'm sooooo bored! B-O-R-E-D. BORED! BORED! BORED!

"On earth as it is in Heaven."

I wonder if Julie Andrews and I will be friends in heaven. I loved her in *Mary Poppins*. I really liked that bag of hers. All that stuff just kept coming out!

"Give us this day, our daily bread . . . "

I'm so hungry, I could puke. I sure hope they don't have Sloppy Joes today. Those were gross! Maybe we'll have hot dogs. I'll take mine with ketchup, no mustard. I hate mustard.

"And forgive us our trespasses, as we forgive those who trespass against us."

What the heck is a trespass anyway? And why should I care if someone tresses past me?

"And lead us not into temptation but deliver us from evil . . . "

I am so tempted to short-sheet Sally's bed. That would serve her right for stealing the top bunk.

"For Thine is the kingdom and the power and the glory forever."

This hour feels like forever. FOR-E-VERRRR!

Amen.

There. I prayed. Now what?

I thumbed through my Bible, not sure what to look for. Then I remembered something about confession, so I called up all the sins I could think of. I asked God's forgiveness for being jealous of my perfect sister. I apologized for spending part of my tithe money on the new Monkees album. And I confessed my bad attitude about having to sit in the dirt and pray for a whole stinkin' hour *when I'd rather be swimming*! This last offense served to usher in a repeat practice I would later dub Prayer Guilt. In the years to come I would amass vast reservoirs of this guilt. But on that hot summer's day long ago at Camp Nunny Cha Ha, I simply shrugged it off as I raced toward the mess hall.

As I mentioned earlier, I grew up in church. We lived in the suburbs but attended a large metropolitan church in the heart of downtown Tulsa. And when I say we attended, I mean that we were there Sunday morning, Sunday night, Wednesday evening, and an occasional Friday night and/or Saturday for socials, choir rehearsals, banquets, revivals, or mission endeavors. We never missed. I'm pretty sure my parents borrowed their church attendance creed from postal workers because neither snow nor rain nor heat nor gloom of night could keep us from driving twenty-something miles to and from our beloved church.

Not that I minded. I loved going to church. All my best friends were there. We loved hanging out in that mammoth old building that occupied an entire city block. In fact, my earliest crushes were on boys at church. Granted, some of them never even knew I existed, but that's beside the point. I could tune out every word of the sermon and spend the better part of the church service hour just staring across the balcony at Marcus. Then Rod. Then Steve. Oh yeah. *Steve . . .*

But somewhere along the line, I began to equate church attendance with being "spiritual." And since we never missed, I figured I was quite the spiritual girl. Each week when I turned in my offering envelope, I checked off all those little boxes to show that I'd read my Bible, memorized a verse of scripture, prayed, gave an offering and attended worship service. For which I was awarded stars on a chart gracing our Sunday school door. That was me—Chrissy Christian, with the perfect attendance record to prove it.

And let's not overlook the Bible. Over the years I was given a series of different Bibles. I loved having my own Bible with my name stamped in gold right there on the front cover. I had Bibles illustrated with color pictures of favorite Bible stories. Others with red letters to represent any words that came out of Jesus' mouth. Soft leather Bibles. Hardcover Bibles with spines that eventually cracked. Tiny New Testaments to slip into my purse. Even a far-out, groovy edition in the 1960s with psychedelic lettering on the front. Years later, when I grew up and started going to more in-depth Bible studies, it was all about the underlining, highlighting, and even an elaborate system of shading with colored pencils those passages we studied in class. My favorite Bible was one I purchased about fifteen years ago. Soft brown leather exterior with extra-wide margins on each page that gave me plenty of room to make notes or jot down questions. Yes, that's me—Bible Barbie.

Amidst all the camp experiences, years of faithfully attending church every time the doors were open, and collecting all kinds of Bibles, I know we must have studied prayer. I'm sure many a Sunday school lesson addressed the subject.

From an early age we learned to pray out loud in class. We were uncomfortable doing it, but we quickly learned that the shorter the prayer, the faster we'd get out of class. *Thank-you-God-for-this-day-and-bless-the-missionaries-and-heal-the-sick-amen.* And we were outta there!

Going Through the Motions

Still, as the years drifted by, for me it was all about the mechanics of prayer and Bible study and going to church. My motivations were all wrong, of course. But if I'm completely honest, I have to admit that very little seemed to sink in. I was in full-blown spoon-feed mode. I was much too caught up in playing the part of a Christian to be concerned with the depth of my spiritual life. Occasionally a crisis would pop up on the horizon, and I would pray as hard as I could. But God wasn't fooled by my emergency-mode prayers. I could almost imagine Him saying, "How come you never talk to Me unless you're in some kind of trouble?" A valid point, considering I'd basically ignored Him Monday through Saturday. Okay, and most of Sunday too.

During my college years, I went through some rough waters. I turned my back on God and decided to have some fun. I'm not going to share my dirty laundry and tell you any of the juicy details. Not gonna happen. Let's just say I came to a fork in the road and chose the road more traveled. Not proud of it, but there it is. As I look back on those years, I have plenty of regrets. But God's amazing grace was there waiting for me when I finally grew up and willingly "put away childish things" (1 Corinthians 13:11*b*, NKJV).

A few years down the road, God blessed me with the most patient and wonderful husband on the face of the earth.

Not only is Ken my husband, he's my best friend. We have two kids I could brag on *ad nauseam.* Hannah and Ben are the joy of our lives, and we couldn't be more proud of them.

Entwined in those early years of marriage and starting a family, Ken finished seminary and began his ministerial career at a large church in Naples, Florida. We were there for five incredible years before leaving to serve at a church just three hours north in the St. Petersburg/Clearwater area. I'd always dreamed of living near the beach, and initially we loved living in the Sunshine State. We also loved the congregations and fellow staff members and their families.

A Spiritual Detour

But Ken's tenure in church ministry didn't end on a very happy note. Years after the fact, it's easy to look back and see the hand of God through that long journey. But at the time? Not so much. Ken handled the whole situation with complete integrity and character. I'd always known he was an incredible man, but never before had I realized what a godly man he was. Like the biblical story of Daniel, Ken came through the fire, which didn't destroy him but only made him stronger. I was so proud of him. I still am.

I'd like to tell you Ken's wife (that would be me) came through the same fire with unfathomable grace, but that would be a lie. A great big fat whale of a lie. I was a train wreck, both emotionally and spiritually. I wasn't angry at God, but my relationship with Him got caught in the undertow. For a season I wanted nothing to do with church. I'd had enough church to last a lifetime, thank you very much.

And as the months drifted by, I became more and more cynical about anything and everything remotely "Christian." I got angry at pompous television preachers and their ridiculous gimmickry, not to mention their creepy wives with big, big hair and clown-like make-up. I judged many of them as outright frauds. (For the record, time would reveal several of these "ministers" were nothing more than con artists.)

I also became critical of what I called the "merchandising" of Christianity—a market saturated with WWJD wrist bands, *"Jesus Loves Me"* coffee mugs, *Prayer of Jabez* coasters, and John 3:16 bumper stickers. (In the spirit of complete transparency, I should probably mention a line of products my husband suggested we merchandise upon hearing I had sold the book you now hold in your hands. He came up with rain-worthy Slacker Slickers, comfy Slacker Slippers, tasty Slacker Crackers (unleavened, of course), and even a companion prayer journal we'd call the Slacker Prayer Packer. Well, you get the idea. Coming soon to a flea market near you.)

Then God opened the door for us to move to Tennessee, something I'd wanted to do for several years. My sister and her family lived near Nashville, and we couldn't wait to move there. We found a beautiful house surrounded by an acre and a half of wooded trees. I felt at home, back in a place that enjoyed all four seasons instead of just one.

Let me backtrack for a moment. There's an old saying that goes, "Whenever one door closes, another one opens." Then there's the Christianese version that says, "When God closes a door, He always opens a window." Those kinds of saccharine-sweet clichés normally gag me. But I have to say that we are living proof of this particular concept.

In what can only be considered an outright miracle, God provided an income for us after Ken lost his job at our church in Florida. Ken had been mentoring a church member who had created a company that provided Internet filtering for computers, providing a way to block pornography. When Remington decided he didn't want to pursue the day-to-day demands his new company required, he literally offered the company to Ken, free and clear, if he wanted it. Cynic that I was at the time, even I could see that God had provided for us in a bold and miraculous way. Ken was able to work from our home, which allowed him to stay closely involved during our kids' teen years. When you serve on a church staff, especially large metropolitan churches, you rarely have an evening at home with the family. This was a welcomed change that Ken and the kids and I loved.

So there we were—handed a dream job on a silver platter, living in a place we loved, thrilled to have Ken at home with us, and finally available to share in every fraction of our family life again. Sounds like heaven on earth, right? Then why was I still so miserable?

To help us get on our feet financially while Ken's company began to grow, I took a job those first couple of years in Tennessee. It was a good job in a Christian company where I worked alongside some wonderful people. But I hadn't worked outside the home for more than fifteen years, and I felt completely suffocated. I packed on a hefty number of unwanted pounds, which only added to my misery. And I noticed a snarky attitude creeping into every pore of my being. Not since the dark days of peri-menopause had I known such consuming angst and frustration. I was such a mess, I cried myself to sleep on December 31, 1999, while the rest of the world celebrated the arrival of a new millennium.

I couldn't seem to shake the depression. I have no idea how Ken put up with me during those years. I butted heads constantly with our daughter and felt a growing distance with our son. But I knew no one was to blame but me. They were just kids—teenagers trying out their wings of independence. Now, when I read back through my journals of those rocky times, I wonder why my family didn't just put me in a strait-jacket and check me into someplace called Sunnydale or Happy Hills. Somewhere in a galaxy far, far away.

What's especially peculiar to me as I think back on this time in my life is the fact that I never stopped to realize my depression and frustration might stem from a spiritual problem. I've told you before I've been a Christian almost my entire life. I'd studied the Bible and attended church and all those other things good Christians do. But none of it seemed to matter anymore.

In fact, I'll admit to you here and now, I was extremely bitter. Bitter on so many different levels in so many different areas of my life. It was eating me alive. I recently heard someone call bitterness "a self-imposed prison cell." I was not only locked behind bars in my self-imposed prison, I had set up housekeeping there. I had furnished my cell with resentment, regret, jealousy, failure, and pure, high-octane bitterness.

I was also beginning to wonder where God was in all of this. Yes, I'd seen His hand in our move to Tennessee and the job He'd provided for Ken. But my attempts at prayer seemed to bounce off the ceiling. And please—don't quote me those lines from "Footprints in the Sand" or the lyrics of songs of faith. I've sung them all, I've memorized the verses, and I know the facts. I just couldn't understand why God wasn't there for me when in my heart I knew He was supposed to be.

Chapter 2

My Journey Continues

I was crying to the LORD with my voice,
And He answered me from His holy mountain.
—PSALM 3:4, NASB

efore I continue, I have to offer another word of caution. In no way, shape, or form do I suggest that what I'm about to tell you is good theology. Not even close. But it's so pivotal to my journey, there's no way to exclude it if I'm to be transparent with my testimony. So here goes. On March 29, 2003, I wrote the following on the first page of a new journal:

> Lord,
> Today I ask you with all my heart to help me make a new start in my prayer life. I ask Your forgiveness for my negligence in my walk with You. With this new day and this fresh page, please help me make You and make prayer a priority once again.
>
> Father, I need You. And I need Your help. I'm committing to meet You here every day. Please strengthen me, especially in my discipline, and fill me with the desire to draw close to You. Forgive my apathy, and draw me back to You.

As honestly as I know how, I open my heart to you and ask You to come in once again. Renew my passion for You, Lord. Help me dust off my Bible and reconnect.

I know what you're thinking. *Whoa, what a committed Christian. How bold! How spiritual! You can almost hear the angels singing in heaven!* What a beautiful, heartfelt prayer. Isn't it, though? There's just one thing wrong with it. What I actually felt, deep in the dark recesses of my heart, what I didn't dare put down on paper, is the following.

God, I'm tired of playing this game, this so-called "walk" with You. I'm so sick of my life and my failed attempts to be genuine and real, that I'm ready to throw down the gauntlet. I'll keep my promise to meet with You every single day for a week. If, at the end of the week, I can see a real difference in my life, then I'll commit to another week. Then another after that. For as long as it takes. But if spending time with You for the next seven days in a row does NOT improve my life or affect any kind of change in my heart and my walk with You, then I'm over it. I'm done.

Ouch. You have no idea how painful it is to see those words in print. But there they are. Whenever I think back about it, I see this image of me shaking my freckled little fist at God. Can you imagine? Even now, it sends a shiver down my spine—the audacity to say such a thing to Almighty God. It's a wonder I wasn't struck by lightning.

And then I visualize something else. Times in my life as a mother when one of my kids would be so angry with me, they'd yell, "I hate you! I hate you! I hate you!" or "I can't wait to leave this house and never come back!" Words spoken in white-hot anger that always cooled—eventually. In my heart I knew my child didn't really mean those words. I'd said them to my own mother a few times. Still, to hear them from the mouth of my own child—a child I'd brought into this world and nurtured and cherished and loved—to hear such words always left a wound in my heart. How much deeper the pain we inflict on our loving Father when our words pierce His heart and our actions betray Him.

Of course, I'd always been taught that God grants us His mercy and His love even when we don't deserve it. And for the record, none of us do. Just to think He would respond as He did to my pathetic, bratty outburst? Unthinkable. But my heavenly Father showed up in ways I couldn't have imagined; in ways that could only be explained as coming from the One who loved me unconditionally. He knew my dreams and the desires of my heart (after all, He put them there), so He knew precisely where and how to get my undivided attention.

God Revealed Himself to Me

At the time, I'd been working on a novel for several months, but I'd hit a brick wall. A big one. Not long after that first week's challenge to God, I began to notice those bricks falling away. In fact, the story was pouring itself into my head so fast I could barely keep up as I pounded my keyboard. What a rush! I'd also been waiting anxiously to hear from several publishers and agents I'd submitted other projects to. Patience is not one of my virtues, as you've probably guessed by now. I had almost given up hope of ever hearing from any of them. Then, a couple of weeks later, I got a contract from an agent. I couldn't believe it. But even in my still-fragile state of mind and renewed walk with God, I knew exactly who to thank. Finally. Finally! I was going to see my dream come true! It was just the break I needed at the precise moment I needed it. Who but God could have pulled that together?

One day in the midst of that first week, I was browsing the book section of a local store. I'm a serious coffee-lover, so when I spotted the picture of a coffee cup and saucer on a book entitled *Fresh-Brewed Life: A Stirring Invitation to Wake Up Your Soul*[1] I grabbed a copy. I didn't know it at the time, but God used that alluring book cover to place a life-changing book in my hands. I devoured that book. Or, should I say, I *drank in* that book? I couldn't put it down. I loved it so much, I raced back to the store to buy more copies, but they'd sold out. I went online, ordering copies to send some of my closest friends and family.

What was so special about *Fresh-Brewed Life* (hereafter referred to as FBL)? The author, Nicole Johnson, is a gifted communicator both in print and in front of live audiences. I loved her self-deprecating sense of humor and her ability to dig deep to mine precious pearls of wisdom that remind us of God's profound love for each one of us. But apart from all that, it became obvious that God led me to *that* book, in *that* particular week, to speak to me in a specific way. Let me show you an example. During that first week, I wrote this entry in my prayer journal.

> I read an amazing chapter today in FBL about the voices we hear in our heads from the enemy; how they fill us with negativity and hopelessness and hold us back from reaching for our dreams. God reminded me to banish those voices and tune in to

HIS voice. Moments later, while reading in the Psalms, these verses jumped off the page at me: "Make me to hear joy and gladness . . . Restore unto me the joy of thy salvation" (Psalm 51:8,12, KJV). These were the words of God, the voice I've longed to hear!

The next day's entry.

"What you are passionate about was created in you to make a splash in this life that no one else can make. Make it. Make it now."[2] Never once have I ever realized the truth of that statement. Me? Making a splash no one else can make? Thank You, God! How I needed to hear that today!

And the next.

Today, Nicole hit a nerve. She talked about dealing with disappointment through what she called "spectator living"—when, rather than follow our dreams and longings, we don't even try, so we won't be disappointed . . . "We never pause long enough to listen to our dreams, so we don't have to be responsible for them . . . If we don't wish or dream, we aren't disappointed. If we aren't disappointed, we can tolerate our lives."[3]

I have to ask myself how long I've been living like this? Lord, I feel like I'm at a crossroads in my life. Like there's a huge "NOW WHAT?" sign standing in front of me. Will I live the second half of my life just drifting along, full of regrets and disappointments? The thought of that nauseates me.

Those thoughts sent me on a quest to discover my dreams and goals, sort of a Bucket List of things to do before I die. Realistic dreams and goals, but also those that might stretch me out of my comfort zone. By the start of week 6, here's what I wrote in my journal.

> I'm noticing a thrill unlike anything I've ever experienced before. Lord, since I've started this challenge to meet You faithfully every day, I find I have more ideas and things I want to do than I'll ever be able to do in my lifetime. And it feels WONDERFUL! Thank You, Lord. But what do I do with all of these ideas? Where do I go from here? I'm practically giddy with all these things bouncing around in my head!

Giddy? *Moi?* How did I go from near despair—threatening to walk away from my faith in God forever—to giddy? I realized there could be only one explanation: God. He made good on His promise to love me, warts and all, and He showed up to meet me where I was—bitter and exhausted and spiritually out of gas. I offered Him seven days, He offered me unconditional love for all eternity. And for the first time in my life, I realized it was okay to place value on all that He made me to be.

I realized I was worthy of His love because He made me in His own image! Sure, I'd known these things in my head, but I'd never believed them with my heart. Accepting this unconditional love in my heart made a huge difference in my life.

The freedom I discovered on this journey has manifested itself over and over and over again. I could pull hundreds of excerpts from my prayer journals and fill every page of this book, giving so many examples of the ways God has touched my heart, restoring me to my salvation.

But enough about me. Now it's your turn.

Let's roll up our sleeves and find out how to get you started on *your* prayer journey. Even before you turn this page, be assured I'm praying for you to catch the thrill and joy of meeting God one-on-one, every day. I pray it becomes as necessary to your daily life as breathing. I pray it becomes such a significant part of your life that you can't imagine how you ever lived without it.

Ready? Let's do it!

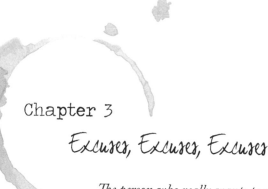

Chapter 3

Excuses, Excuses, Excuses

The person who really wants to do something finds a way; the other person finds an excuse.
—AUTHOR UNKNOWN

How about we have a little fun? Let's take off the kid gloves, stop beating around the bush, lay all our cards on the table, get right to the point, leave no stone unturned, start firing on all cylinders, and tackle the whole enchilada. Every writer worth his salt (oops, there goes another one) knows that clichés are considered a lazy and tacky form of writing. The Cliché Police may chase us down, but isn't it cathartic to fling a few of these forbidden fruits around? In other words, in the spirit of unfettered laziness, let's take a whimsical look at some of the silly reasons we don't pray.

Almost every book I've read on the subject of prayer has a chapter on excuses. Most of them deal with deeply spiritual matters of the heart. But since you and I are just now getting acquainted, I thought we might take a different approach and spice it up with a hint of humor. An ice-breaker, if you will. How better to cut to the chase? Sorry. That one slipped.

The Top 10 Excuses Why Christians Don't Pray

10. *I have bad knees. I can't kneel to pray. It doesn't count if I'm not kneeling.* Talk about your lame excuse.

 9. *My pastor prays at church services. That's enough for me.* Piggy-back prayer coverage. Who knew?

 8. *God's got His hands full with tsunamis and people living in poverty and starvation and wars and hospital wards and crime and—well, face it. He doesn't have time for my piddlysquat prayers.* Be not downhearted, my friend. There are no "piddlysquat" prayers to God. "He's got the whole world in His hands"—feel free to sing along—"He's got the whole world . . ."

 7. *It's none of your business. It's personal. It's just between God and me.* Sounds like someone woke up with a case of the grumpies. Here, have some coffee. We'll chat later. After your second cup, okay?

 6. *If God knows me so well, I shouldn't have to verbalize my prayers for Him. He's either omniscient or He's not.* Come on now, don't be shy. Tell us what you really think.

 5. *Prayer is a waste of time. It doesn't change a thing. I know— I prayed for a pony when I was a kid and never got one. Then I prayed for world peace. Fat chance of that ever happening.* I'm not psychic, but I'm guessing you'd say that glass of water you're holding is half empty. Am I right?

 4. *I can never stay focused. My mind wanders. I figure that's an insult to God, so I'm better off if I don't pray at all.* Are you going to eat that chocolate donut or can I have it? I'm sorry, what were you saying?

3. *I don't know what to say. I don't know how. It's just too awkward.* Well, so was learning how to go potty when you were two, but you kept after it and chances are, you're no longer in diapers. *Please* tell me you're not still in diapers?

2. *I'm lazy. There. I said it. Satisfied?* Yes! And doesn't it feel good to come clean? Oh, that the rest of us should be so honest.

And the number 1 excuse Christians give for not praying?

1. *I Don't Have Time! I'm Busy!* Yeah, I heard that about you. Is it true the world will indeed stop spinning on its axis if you don't keep all your appointments today? Just curious.

I have plenty to say about this number 1 jewel, but I'll save it for Chapter 5. In the meantime, let's address some of the previous countdown excuses.

To Kneel or Not to Kneel, That Is the Question

Hopefully, you're not serious about this one because I tossed it in just for fun. I'm unaware of any scripture requiring us to get down on our knees to pray. I grew up in a Southern Baptist church, and the only time we knelt for prayer was in response to an altar call at the end of the service or following a particularly fiery sermon by a visiting evangelist. Our pews weren't equipped with the pull-down kneeling bench found in most Catholic and Episcopalian churches.

But that doesn't mean I never knelt to pray. To be honest, I never even gave it much thought until the last few years. I realized there were certain occasions when Christ knelt to pray, and I began asking God if He wanted me on my knees. No, I never heard an audible voice. But sometimes, when I'd notice my mind drifting in the midst of my prayer time, I sensed an internal nudge in my spirit urging me to get down on my knees. It immediately helped me to focus on God and obliterate the distractions. I try to stay tuned in for those holy nudges so I don't miss the blessing.

Piggy-back Prayers

You don't have to be a Mother Teresa to know this one won't cut it. Unfortunately, even though most of us would never admit it, we convince ourselves that a few minutes warming the pew now and then, listening to someone else pray is somehow sufficient. As if by showing up and tipping our spiritual hat to God, we're covered. News flash: God wants *you*. He wants a relationship with you. That's why He made you. And I have to be honest with you here. If you don't have much interest in spending time with God, I have to wonder about your salvation. No, I'm not Judge Judy. But if you're just going through the motions, playing the part but never owning your relationship with God, chances are you need to go back to square one and be sure beyond a shadow of doubt that you truly gave your heart to God. So you can know that you know that you know that Jesus is Lord of your life. If you didn't previously make a pit stop there, flip over to the back of the book to the section I mentioned earlier about becoming a Christian. Go on. Take your time. I'll wait for you.

God's Got Bigger Problems than Me.

Sure He does. But remember those "O" words we use in reference to God? I'm referring to *omniscient* (having total knowledge of all things) and *omnipresent* (being present everywhere at the same time). These are two attributes of God that are tough for us to comprehend. But as believers, we accept that God is certainly capable of knowing everything and being everywhere simultaneously. To think otherwise would be to question who He says He is. And that's never a smart choice, Mr. Doubting Thomas.

One of my favorite books is *Just Give Me Jesus* by Anne Graham Lotz, daughter of beloved evangelist Billy Graham. I heard Anne speak several years ago at a conference in Florida and was literally blown away. I'm not sure I've ever heard anyone speak with such depth of understanding about our walk as Christians. I remember thinking how refreshing it was to hear her message because she was so incredibly genuine. There wasn't an ounce of insincerity in her. There wasn't a single moment when she came across as a celebrity or some much-sought-after speaker on the Christian circuit. When she spoke, we felt the presence of the Lord in that room. Not long after that event, I picked up a copy of her book *Just Give Me Jesus.* I've read it over and over as part of my prayer time for years. Let me share what she says about God's interest in us.

> The greatness of His power to create and design and form and mold and make and build and arrange defies the limits of our imagination. And since He created everything, there is nothing beyond His power to fix or mend or heal or restore. . . . Having brought everything into existence that exists, He has never become bored with or distracted from or unconcerned about His creation. The Living Logos personally hovers over all He has created, giving it His full attention.[1]

In other words, *nothing* is too small for God. There is nothing in your life or mine that He regards as "piddlysquat." Are we clear on that now?

It's Personal.

Now I have to agree with this one. Prayer is designed to be personal because it is the form of communication between you and your Father in heaven. In Matthew 6, Christ gave us a model for prayer. We know it as the Lord's Prayer. But skip back a few verses and listen to what He says.

> But when you pray, do not be like the hypocrites, for they love to pray standing in the synagogues and on the street corners to be seen by men. I tell you the truth, they have received their reward in full. When you pray, go into your room, close the door and pray to your Father, who is unseen. Then your Father, who sees what is done in secret, will reward you.
>
> —Matthew 6:5-6

God isn't fooled for a millisecond by those who pray loud and long and with great braggadocios for the sake of being heard. You've heard those kinds of prayers and so have I. It's like listening to a staged performance worthy of an Oscar nomination rather than the heartfelt prayer of a humble believer. *Dear Gaaaaaaahhhhhhhdddddd.* . . . Oh, please. Give it a rest. We are not impressed. Or the ones who seem to turn on tears at will. I have nothing against those who are sincerely passionate or emotional about something they're sharing. But to those whose tears run like a faucet on some arbitrary timer, cued to start the water-works at a given point in every sermon? Sorry. Not buying it.

Preachers come in all shapes and sizes and flavors. Some are dry as the Sahara, some are funny, some are excitable, some are readers. But the one thing I do not want to see behind the pulpit is an actor. Leave the theatrics at home, Pastor. Just be real.

Thankfully, God is far more interested in what's in your heart. That's why He beckons us to pray in private. He's telling us to get rid of all the fluff, the flowery language, and anything else that might hinder us from pouring out our hearts before Him—and from listening to what He tells us in return.

> And when you pray, do not keep on babbling like pagans, for they think they will be heard because of their many words. Do not be like them, for your Father knows what you need before you ask him.
> —Matthew 6:7-8

Speaking of babbling, you've heard enough of mine for now. How about we continue our discussion of excuses in the next chapter?

Chapter 4

More Excuses?

> *He that is good for making excuses*
> *is seldom good for anything else.*
> —BENJAMIN FRANKLIN

Oy vey! What a list we have going! Now, where were we?

God is omniscient. He knows what I'm going to pray
before I even think it, much less say it.

True. You're spot on. But this reminds me of that old joke about the wife who complained to her husband on their fiftieth anniversary, "Why don't you ever tell me you love me?" Her husband answered, "I told you the day I married you. Nothing's changed. If it does, I'll let you know." Paging Dr. Phil. We've found your next guest for your show.

Do you know why God created humans in the first place? I mean, stop and think about it for a moment. He's *God*. He can have or create anything in the heavens He wants. I'm sure the holy refrigerator is packed solid with cartons of Blue Bell ice cream—times a million. All those amazing flavor combinations minus the calories and fat grams, of course. We are, after all, talking about heaven here. Amen? Then again, heaven is so far beyond our comprehension that to yearn for earthly things like ice cream is kind of silly. Even Blue Bell's Banana Pudding ice cream or Blackberry Cobbler ice cream probably tastes bland in comparison to the phenomenal foods that await us in heaven. There will be food in heaven, right? Please tell me there will be food. Anyone?

Here's the point. God needs only to think it, and anything He needs and wants is at His disposal. So He certainly didn't need us, which can only mean one thing: He must have wanted us. Why? I did a quick study of the scriptures on that exact question. Oddly enough—wannabe Bible scholar that I am—I didn't find an exact answer to that question. But Genesis 2:7 tells us: "And the LORD God formed man of the dust of the ground and breathed into his nostrils the breath of life, and man became a living being." Unlike the rest of His creation, God gave humans a living soul. That much we know.

Then, in Genesis 2:18, we read: "The LORD God said, 'It is not good for the man to be alone. I will make a helper suitable for him.'" Whoa, did you catch that? Right there, we can sneak a glimpse into God's heart. He's concerned that Adam would be too lonely without someone to relate to. He made Adam, after all. He knew that there was a vacuum in Adam's heart without a companion, someone to do life with. Could it be this is our clue revealing God's omniscient awareness of our need for relationship?

You know the rest of the story. Knowing Adam would be freaked if God just reached down and took a rib from his side (ouch?), the Creator introduced the first recorded use of anesthesia and BAM! He knocked Adam out, sending him into a deep sleep.

Verse 22 says, "Then the LORD God made a woman from the rib he had taken out of the man, and he brought her to the man." I don't know about you, but I'm guessing Adam had the shock of his lifetime when he woke up and took a look at Eve. "Whoa! Who are you, and what did you do with my rib?" Actually, I'm guessing it was probably more like, "Whoa, baby! Now that's what I'm talking about!" Can't you just see the two of them checking each other out? (Am I the only one blushing here?) Somehow I think Adam was ridiculously happy to see Eve, and vice versa, don't you? And they didn't even know what was in store for them. They just knew it was nice not to be alone.

The point is, God understands our desire for companionship. How so? It's not that big a leap to realize He understands that desire because He above all has that same desire! If you read ahead in Genesis 3:8, it says, "Then the man and his wife heard the sound of the LORD God as he was walking in the garden in the cool of the day." God took a walk in the garden, knowing Adam and Eve were there. He wanted to be with them! Unfortunately, they'd just bitten off more than they could chew (so to speak) and committed *the sin* that would affect all of humankind throughout the rest of history (Genesis 2:16-17). So what did they do? They ran off and hid. Like God couldn't find them? Adam. Eve. What were you thinking?

It was that choice that got them in trouble. Yes, God could have created robotrons, automatically wired to be perfect, make no mistakes, and readily equipped to be in a relationship with Him. But that would never do. God wanted us to want that relationship of our own free will. So He gave us a choice: either to follow Him and have a personal relationship with Him, or to reject Him.

Scottish-born minister and teacher Oswald Chambers put it this way.

The most important aspect of Christianity is not the work we do, but the relationship we maintain and the surrounding influence and qualities produced by that relationship.[1]

How's that for a big picture? Merely by making that faith choice to follow Him, each one of us have the astounding opportunity to become a vessel of His love to the world around us. Are you getting this? Do you realize the magnitude of your relationship with God? Probably not. Because if we truly got it at the very core of our being, we'd have no problem understanding the depth of the relationship God offers to us and we would run with it. My question to you is this: What's keeping you from running with it? Hmm?

So you prayed for a pony and didn't get one, proving once and for all that prayer is a waste of time.

Maybe yours wasn't a prayer for a pony; but, more than likely, at some point in your life you've prayed for something you didn't get. My pastor, Pete Wilson, gave a message on prayer, specifically citing this idea many of us have that prayer is a kind of transaction. Beside him on the platform, an object the size of a refrigerator stood cloaked beneath a black cover. He said, "Most of us have reduced prayer down to a transaction. A way to manipulate what we want. A vending machine."[2] At that point, he yanked off the cover revealing a large vending machine, loaded with all kinds of snacks. He inserted some coins and pushed the button for peanut M&Ms (smart man, my pastor). Nothing happened. He hit the machine a couple of times, tried to rock it. Nothing.

He continued. "Most of the time when we go to God, it's because we want something. If we get what we want, we turn and walk off, satisfied. If we don't get what we want, we get frustrated; we kick the machine and blame God for not answering our request."[3]

Pete warned that this "transaction" view of prayer will always disappoint us because at the root of it, we think it's all about us.[4] But prayer is so much more than giving God a list of our wants and needs or, in some cases, our demands. Prayer is communication. It's talking and listening.

Let's look at another Oswald Chambers quote.

> "Your Father knows the things you have need of before you ask Him" (Matthew 6:8). Then why should we ask? The point of prayer is not to get answers from God, but to have perfect and complete oneness with Him. If we pray only because we want answers, we will become irritated and angry with God. We receive an answer every time we pray, but it does not always come in the way we expect, and our spiritual irritation shows our refusal to identify ourselves truly with our Lord in prayer. We are not here to prove that God answers prayer, but to be living trophies of God's grace.[5]

"To have perfect and complete oneness with Him." I love that. Can you even imagine what our lives would be like if we aspired to that kind of oneness with God?! How often have we settled for mediocrity because we've never really understood this basic truth that prayer is communication? How many times have we shunned God because our M&Ms didn't drop down after we inserted our coins?

Let's dig even deeper. If you were handed a printed transcript of all your prayers to God over the last week or month or even a year, what would it look like? Chances are it would be a repetitive list of give me this, give me that, gimme-gimme-gimme. When I think about the times I've been stuck in these "gimme" prayers, I can actually imagine the expression on Jesus' face as I blab on and on about gimme-this and gimme-that. I can see Him rolling his eyes, unsuccessfully stifling a yawn as He shakes His head. Finally He drops His head back and closes His eyes.

Okay, okay, I'm sure He has way more patience than that. But by now you know I'm a visual person. It helps me to picture Him that way when I get carried away with myself. And face it. When we spend our whole prayer time uttering nothing more than a long laundry list of gimmes, we sound like a bunch of spoiled brats, don't we? Guess what? We are. But we're hardly alone. Most of us probably have similar if not identical transcripts because we've never moved beyond our childish motives.

The fact is, God always answers our prayers. He just doesn't necessarily answer them the way we expect them. My husband always speaks of God's perspective toward our lives using the illustration of a parade. If we're riding along the parade route, we can see what's just ahead of us and what's just behind us. That's it. But the TV reporter way up in the helicopter sees the route from start to finish. And that's how God sees our life's journey. He's got the view from the Holy Blimp. He can see what lies in the path directly ahead of us and waaaaaay beyond. So when we pray, He answers each prayer with our best long-term interest in mind. He may say no, He might say yes, or He may tell us to hold our horses and wait. Our challenge is to accept his response and trust Him—completely.

Oh, and one more thing. About that prayer for world peace? God gave us a roadmap for that long, long ago. It's called the Ten Commandments. Check out Exodus, chapter 20. That about covers it.

> *I can never stay focused. My mind wanders. I figure that's an insult to God, so I'm better off if I don't pray at all.*

Ah, a case of PADD. Prayer Attention Deficit Disorder. Happens to all of us, my friend. But rather than give up, get help. Get organized! I promise if you'll make the effort to rein in that mind of yours, even for just a few minutes each day, you'll start to see a difference. In Chapter 7 I'll give you some specific tools that will help tremendously. But for now, let me share my favorite verse in the Bible. It's my life's verse. Are you ready for this? "Draw near to God and He will draw near to you" (James 4:8, NKJV).

Stop right there. Read it again. Can you hear God calling out to you in those eleven words? Can you even comprehend the promise He's offering you? Unlike the empty promises and meaningless words of today's culture, God doesn't mince words or spill out fluff. He is good to His word. And He's reaching out to you. He's promising to respond personally if you'll only draw near to Him.

I've loved that verse for over twenty years, and it still gives me goose bumps whenever I think about it. Here's another verse along the same lines: "You will seek me and find me when you seek me with all your heart" (Jeremiah 29:13).

Take Him at His word. Don't give up. Don't miss the blessing!

> *I'm lazy. There. I said it. Satisfied?*

Pssst. Wanna know a secret? If you strip away all the excuses we dish up to God day after day, you'll find they all come down to this: laziness. It may show up in different disguises, especially when we're trying so hard to hide it. Hiding from God? See previous Adam and Eve reference above. Enough said?

We are a lazy people when it comes to spending time with God. Wouldn't you agree? If so, what does that say about you and me? But admitting it and doing something about it are two different things. In the following pages, I'm going to challenge you to arm yourself with all the ammo you need to blast those lazy germs to smithereens. Which I think is somewhere near South Dakota. Come on, Rambo and Ramboettes, let's go for it!

Chapter 5
Our Number 1 Excuse for Not Praying

I don't have time to pray!
I'm too busy!

I t's only fitting that our number 1 excuse for not praying should have a chapter all to itself. And while I still contend that laziness is at the root of this excuse as well, I also believe our lifestyles morph this particular strain of laziness into a generally accepted excuse in today's culture. Somehow we've equated "busyness" with accomplishment and success. I've had many friends over the years who routinely call and list all they've done by eight in the morning. I'm sure I'm supposed to be impressed, but usually I just roll over and go back to sleep. Makes me yawn just thinking about it.

What is behind this frantic pace of our everyday lives? It seems to be the inescapable way of life in twenty-first century America. Unfortunately, I think Christians are among the worst offenders. In addition to being a husband or wife, parent, student, employee or employer, friend, volunteer, relative, neighbor, and all those other hats we keep piled on our heads, there's all that busyness of church. Services, classes, choir practices, team/committee meetings, church suppers, Sunday school lessons, potlucks, Bible studies—hold on a sec, I've got to catch my breath here—mission weeks, revivals, vacation Bible schools, the annual church picnic, Christmas cantatas, Easter pageants, mission trips abroad, Sunday school socials, food drives, clothing drives, Angel Trees . . . Have I missed anything?

In *Blue Like Jazz* author Donald Miller addresses this subject from a startling perspective.

> I believe the greatest trick of the devil is not to get us into some sort of evil but rather have us wasting time. This is why the devil tries so hard to get Christians to be religious. If he can sink a man's mind into habit, he will prevent his heart from engaging God.[1]

Bingo! How better to sell us a counterfeit faith than to load up our calendars with a thousand church-focused obligations? A sly one, that devil. And churches all over the world fall for it. You've gotta love churches that stress the tremendous importance of the family, but expect members to be at the church five out of seven nights a week. What's wrong with that equation? And where do we get off thinking we're some kind of saint just because we never miss?

We seem to be a nation and a people who rarely slow down. It's as if we don't know how—unless the stress catches up with us, causing any number of maladies like ulcers, heart attacks, hernias, emotional meltdowns (been there, done that), or sheer exhaustion. Who has time for spiritual matters like prayer? In an ideal world, we'd gladly spend half an hour—oh, let's dream big—maybe even an entire hour—reading our Bibles and praying every single day of our lives. Really? A whole hour? Shoot, if that's the case, let's try to see if we can find those sixty minutes that seem to be MIA and

UFMP (Missing in Action and Unavailable for Meaningful Prayer).

Granted, much of your daily routine depends on your age and marital status. As a single, your time at home is primarily your own. Now don't get your knickers in a knot—I know there are exceptions. Perhaps you're a single parent with children in the home. Maybe you're caring for an aging parent, spending all your free time with them. Those situations drastically change the home dynamic. Your time is rarely your own! And if you're married, particularly if children are in the picture, your time must be allocated between your spouse and your children and all the other demands of your life.

No matter what your home life may look like—Norman Rockwell or otherwise—let me ask you a few questions. This morning when you got up, did you spend time reading your favorite blogs? Did you answer e-mails while your coffee was brewing? Did you read the paper while eating your Cocoa Puffs? If you're a guy, did you watch *SportsCenter* on TV while you shaved and got dressed? If you're a woman, did you think through your to do list while you showered this morning, made a pot of coffee before blow-drying your hair, put on your makeup, dressed for work, woke up the kids for school, let the dog out, made breakfast for the family, packed lunches for the kids, and made sure everyone got out the door in time? (Is it just me, or do the guys have the shorter list here? That is so not fair.)

Whoa. I'm worn out just thinking about your mornings. I need a nap.

A word of warning is in order. Unless you're a member of the clergy, I wouldn't recommend having your prayer time once you get to work. Your employer doesn't pay you to spend time with the Lord on the clock. I knew of a woman back in Oklahoma who made quite a show of reading her Bible and praying in the break room after clocking in at work each morning. I'm sure she meant well, but what a terrible witness to her co-workers. Needless to say, her boss eventually showed her the door, and rightly so.

So the morning is gone, you barely have time to grab a bite for lunch, then you're back at work for the afternoon. When you finally head home, you're mentally and/or physically exhausted so you listen to talk radio or a few of your favorite CDs on your homeward commute.

It's now seven in the evening. Regardless if you're single, married, with or without children, you probably have a routine most weeknights. Before you try to assure me you spend your evenings constructively, I should warn you I've done some research. The latest official TV rating stats tell us the average American television viewer is logging more than 153 hours of TV each month. That breaks down to somewhere in the vicinity of five hours per day. And that doesn't even count the additional amount of viewership via the Internet and mobile phones. This tells me there's a pretty good chance you're parked on the couch for hours upon hours of television viewing on a fairly regular basis.

"Yes," you say, "but I'm watching news programming. It's important to know what's happening in the world around us." Yes, my dear news wonk, it is indeed important. Or perhaps you say, "I watch educational stations like the Discovery Channel. Ever watch that show on meerkats? They're fascinating. Practically human!" No kidding. I think I spotted one of my in-laws in last week's episode . . . Personally, the Food Network is my TV drug of choice. Not good for someone who's lived most of her life on a perpetual diet; know what I mean?

But let's face it—whether it's news or educational programming or a string of reality shows or a marathon of sporting events—you're most likely racking up some hefty TV time. Which might explain some of those extra pounds you're totin' around these days. Not that I'm pointing fingers or anything.

By now, it's time for bed. Maybe, upon realizing you haven't had a single blip on your day's radar concerning the Lord, you utter a couple of quick ones as your head hits the pillow. "Lord, forgive me for neglecting You today. Thank You for . . . for . . ." And that about does it. Soon, the snoring commences as you drift off into a blissful sleep, dreaming of meerkats auditioning for *American Idol.*

If I came anywhere close to describing your average day, then chances are you need help. Carving out time to pray doesn't come easy. If you're serious about making your one-on-one time with God a priority, you've got to be willing to tackle that ugly D word: *discipline.* When I think of physical exercise, I can safely say I hate—nay, loathe—the discipline it requires. (Which might explain some of the aforementioned excess pounds I'm carrying around. Ahem.) But discipline is such a necessary part of life. Without it, we waste massive amounts of our time and energy. Likewise, discipline is an integral part of being committed to some form of daily, routine encounter with God.

One of the best books I've read in years is *Second Calling: Finding Passion and Purpose for the Rest of Your Life.* Author Dale Hanson Bourke addresses this matter of our hectic lifestyles: "If I turn up the music of busyness, I will miss the whispers of God's call."[2] Isn't that profound? Over the course of your life, how many of God's whispers have you missed? Does the thought of it break your heart?

Ever hear of the Wesleys? This remarkable eighteenth-century English family played a vital role in the early Christian movement here in America. John Wesley was an Anglican theologian who helped launch the Methodist denomination. His brother Charles, also a leader of that movement, is remembered for penning more than 6,000 hymns, many of the most famous hymns we know today. John and Charles were just two of the *nineteen* children born to Samuel and Susannah Wesley, though nine of their brothers and sisters died as infants, and another was accidentally smothered by a maid. Samuel left Susannah for more than a year after they had an argument over a quite trivial difference of opinion. It must have been one whopper of a fight because he left her alone to care for their ten remaining children with no means of support. But through the many hardships Susannah experienced, she continually grew stronger and more determined to educate her children and raise them to honor God.[3]

Why am I telling you about Susannah Wesley? Because it would have been so easy for her to throw up her hands and cry *why me*?! Instead, this intelligent and strong-willed woman instilled discipline and order in her home. And she did that by maintaining a relentless practice of daily prayer with the Lord. The story is told of many occasions when, unable to find a quiet room for her prayer time, she would flip her apron over her head and pray. Not just for a few minutes, but for *two hours*. She had arranged a system so that the older children would take care of the younger ones during this time. In doing so, they learned first-hand by their mother's example, the importance of a personal prayer life.[4]

It's all about priorities, isn't it? Susannah Wesley had hers in order, that's for sure. Now bear in mind all of the obstacles in her life, then listen to her perspective on the importance of setting aside time to pray each day.

I will tell you what rule I observed when I was young
. . . never to spend more time in mere recreation in
one day than I spent in private religious devotions.[5]

Whoa. Ol' Susannah doesn't beat around the bush, does
she? And to think, she didn't even have the temptation to
watch a weekend marathon of *Law and Order* or play eighteen
holes at Augusta. I wonder what kind of mere recreation was
available to her back then. Needlepoint? Playing the lute?

It's definitely a matter of priorities, but I'd even go a step
further and suggest it's a matter of devotion and adoration.
Let's put it in twenty-first century terms. Imagine this.

You have been summoned by the president of the
United States. (If you don't like the current occu-
pant, make it the last one you did like.) He has
asked you to join him for breakfast at the White
House. His personal secretary called to extend the
invitation to you and give you the details of where
to go and when to be there. The morning arrives.
Your alarm clock buzzes incessantly. As your mind
awakens, you think over your options. Do you—

(A) Throw the alarm clock across the room. As you
begin to drift back to sleep, you vaguely recall
that today is the day you go to the White
House. But you decide it's not that big a deal, so
you blow off the president, snuggle back under
the covers and go back to sleep. Or do you—

(B) Hit the snooze button eight more times then
call his secretary and tell her you're just too
tired and you'll have to take a rain check. She

says the next available date is two years from next week, which suits you fine. Or do you—

(C) Fly out of bed, grab a shower and get dressed, catch up on your correspondence, play a couple rounds of solitaire on your computer, pay some bills, take a long call from a friend while you put dinner in the crock-pot—then look at the clock and realize it's already half an hour past the time you were supposed to be at the White House. You shrug it off and decide you'll get to it another time. Or do you—

(D) Set your alarm clock the night before to wake you earlier than usual. When it goes off, you jump out of bed, shower and dress, then leave the house with plenty of time to spare as you drive to the White House. Graciously and with much anticipation and excitement, you meet the most important person in the world over coffee and croissants. As you and the president began to chat, you think, *I wouldn't have missed this for the world!*

Let me guess. You picked D, didn't you? I know. Maybe I'm psychic after all. I'm also impressed because you certainly know how to respond when summoned by someone important!

Now let's put that scenario in terms of your spiritual life. Your Lord and Savior Jesus Christ has extended a personal invitation for you to join him for a chat—not just today, but *every day of your life.* So what's it going to be? Will you willingly ignore His invitation, throwing your alarm clock across the room, opting for more sleep? Will your good intentions get lost in a flurry of other important tasks? Or will you plan ahead, making sure you don't miss the opportunity of a lifetime—make that eternity—and give your appointed time with your Heavenly Father the priority it deserves?

My goal on these pages is to help you scratch out any response except that last one above. To help you find the joy of meeting God every single day, one-on-one, heart-to-heart, until you reach a point where you can't even imagine starting your day without Him.

How will you make that happen? You already know. That dirty word we discussed a page or so back: *discipline.* Without it, you'll never succeed at much of anything, let alone the habit of spending time with your God.

By now you're saying, "Okay, okay! Prayer requires discipline. I get it! But tell me how do I learn that kind of discipline? Tell me!"

I will. I promise. But first, there's one more thing I need to ask you.

Chapter 6

Just How Badly Do You Want It?

> *But if from there you seek the LORD your God,*
> *you will find Him if you look for him with all*
> *your heart and with all your soul.*
> —DEUTERONOMY 4:29

I want you to be completely honest. No one is looking over your shoulder or breathing down your neck. This is just between you and God, okay? Here's my question.

On a scale of one to ten, how does your "want-to" rank in terms of desiring time to spend with the Lord? How badly do you really want it? If (1) is "I could care less," and (10) is "I cannot imagine starting my day without first spending quality time with God," how do you measure up?

Remember, be as honest as you can. Your word is safe with me. I promise. And I can also guarantee you one thing with absolute certainty: God will do major heart surgery on you if you'll let Him.

So let's determine just how serious you are about your prayer life. Do you sincerely desire a personal, intimate relationship with your Lord? Or is it just lip service and wishful thinking on your part? As believers, we know we're supposed to pray. But knowing and doing aren't even in the same ballpark for most of us. The problem is, if we don't even have the desire to pray, what does that say about us? Imagine being head-over-heels in love with someone—but having no desire whatsoever to spend time with that person. Doesn't sound like a very healthy relationship to me. Exactly what kind of love is that? So when we say we love God, yet make no time for Him in our lives, well—what kind of love is that?

So I'll ask you again. How badly do you want it?

Let's take it one step further. How important is the Lord in the overall scope of your life? What kind of place do you give Him in your daily routine? Remember those "God is my copilot" bumper stickers? Holy screwed-up theology, Batman! That little jewel may be the single most blatantly misconceived product ever to roll out of Christian marketing. When you give your life to God, be assured the last role He wants to play is your copilot. Surrendering to Christ means stepping aside and giving Him the pilot's seat—not the other way around.

Need proof? God is really serious about this. Take another look at the Ten Commandments in Exodus 20. In that coveted number 1 spot, He makes it perfectly clear: "You shall have no other gods before Me." Meaning, you're not the boss of Him! Meaning, you're not the hotshot pilot you think you are, so get your butt over there in the copilot seat and let Him do the flying. Any questions?

Years ago, our youth group performed a dramatic skit I'll never forget. With permission from scriptwriter John Alexander at DramaShare.org, I'd like to share a summary of "The Visitor" with you.

The scene starts with a teenager (we'll call her Briana) sitting in her bedroom. There's a knock at the door. Briana goes to the door, answers it, and finds Jesus (unseen) standing there. She gives Him a big hug, welcomes Him into her room, and invites Him to take a seat on a chair after she clears away all the clutter. She begins a long litany of explanations why she hasn't been able to spend much time with Him lately—homework, Christmas shopping, her busy, busy schedule—and assures Him she's cleared the evening for just the two of them.

Briana tells Jesus all about the things happening in her life. She's been chosen to be captain of the cheerleading squad for next year, and she acknowledges how happy He must surely be since she'll be in such a high profile position—for His honor, of course. She also informs Him she's decided to pursue a career as an airline pilot. That means, unfortunately, that she won't be keeping her promise to serve Him overseas, but that was probably just an unrealistic childish commitment on her part, one He probably knew she'd never keep. She's sure He only wants what's best for her, and she loves that about Him.

Then the phone rings, and Briana is invited to a party that's going on at a friend's house. She hesitates at first, knowing she promised to spend the evening getting caught up with Jesus. But when she finds out a certain guy is there asking for her, she quickly changes her mind. She hangs up and turns to Jesus . . .

"Listen, something has come up; we are going to have to do this later. . . . Some of my friends, they really want me to be with them. And, I thought maybe it would be best, one of Yours being there where many don't even know Your Name."

As Briana gets ready to leave, she tells Jesus she won't be that long. "Listen, why don't You just sit right there 'til I get back. Relax, enjoy! Look, here's a magazine." (Flips through a few pages.) "Well, maybe not this particular magazine . . . wait a minute, television! That's it!" She picks up the remote and starts flipping through the channels." Let's see, what's on tonight? Maybe not that one, what about . . . or maybe. . . . Listen, seems like kind of a nothing night on TV. Silly me." She finally decides Jesus needs to just rest until she returns.

As she starts to leave, it's apparent that Jesus wants to go with her. "Where are You going? You sit down. In the chair, right here. No, You cannot come with me. My friends aren't the type, er, that is, You wouldn't enjoy it at all. See you later then . . ."

He attempts to follow her again. Briana tries to hide her frustration. "I said, You sit! I don't want you to come with me. I mean, I want You, but the time has to be right, understood? And this is simply not the proper time. Stay!"

Once more He starts to follow her. "What gives with You?" she bellows. "I take time out for You, invite You in, then You just try to take over my life! I will tell You when! So back off!"

Again He follows. In utter exasperation, she shouts at Jesus. "I've had it with You! Now then, back there in the corner . . ." Then, one at a time, she lifts His hands and mimes driving nails into them as the sound of hammer blows accompanies each strike. The stages goes black.[1]

I remember the first time I saw that skit. Like everyone else, I thought, what a fool that girl is. Nobody does that to Jesus! It only took a couple of seconds until I felt hot tears streaming down my face. I realized I do the exact same thing every day of my life in a hundred different ways. Oh, maybe not intentionally or as heartlessly as Briana nailing Jesus' hands to the cross. Then again, maybe exactly like that. All those times I leave Him out of my plans, my thoughts, my emotions, my activities. All those times I let the day get away from me without ever stopping to pray. All those times I inadvertently ignore scripture telling me how much He yearns for me to seek Him out. "Taste and see that the LORD is good!" the psalmist said in Psalm 34:8. Jeremiah 33:3 says, "Call to me and I will answer you and tell you great and unsearchable things you do not know." What kind of fool ignores invitations like that?!

The conviction I felt was overwhelming. Still, it's nothing more than hot air and smoke and mirrors if all we do is talk about it, fret over it, or pile on massive amounts of guilt about it.

Anne Graham Lotz tells the story of a man who passed by a pet store and saw a magnificent bird in the window. When he went inside to inquire, he saw a sign on the bird's cage: "This bird is guaranteed to sing." Despite the exorbitant price of $1,000 including the cage, the man had to have the bird; so he paid for it, took the bird in its cage, and went home. He waited all day for the bird to sing, but it never did.

The next morning he went back to the pet store to complain. The clerk apologized for not mentioning that the bird needed a ladder in its cage before it would sing. The man bought the $20 ladder, took it home, put it in the cage—nothing. Each morning he went back to the pet store, angry that the bird still wouldn't sing. And each day the clerk apologized and suggested another necessary item for the cage: a bell for $25, a mirror for $30, a swing for $35. The man stormed home on that last day and put the swing in the cage. The bird climbed its ladder, rang its bell, looked into its mirror, swung on its new swing—then promptly dropped dead!

The man was furious. He grabbed the fully-equipped cage with the dead bird and took it back to the pet store. He yelled at the clerk for selling him a bird for $1,000 and the additional $110 worth of toys. "Not only does this bird not sing," the man roared, "but it's dead! What went wrong?" "Oh," the clerk responded, "did I forget to tell you? He also needed birdseed."[2]

Sound familiar? Have you ever tried to drive your car when the gas gauge reads empty? Ever put on a pair of snow skis and head down the slopes without first learning how to ski? Ever try to fly a military jet without first learning how to fly? Ever attempt brain surgery with no formal medical training? Get the point? How in the world can you live as a Christian if you've never learned how? How can you possibly know the Lord without ever spending time with Him? How can you follow the path He's set before you if you never ask Him which way to go?

But beyond all our mistaken logic and pathetic attempts to make it on our own are the tremendous blessings we miss when we bypass the simple relationship He offers us through prayer.

Since we've already discussed your TV habits, let's use this analogy: Life without prayer is like watching TV on an ancient twelve-inch black-and-white TV set. The picture is snowy and distorted, and no matter how much aluminum foil you wrap around those rabbit ears, you can't see a thing. Life with a personal prayer relationship with God is like watching TV on a sixty-inch flat-screen in high definition, with surround-sound speakers and a picture so clear you think you're right there on the eighteenth hole in Augusta with Mickelson as he makes his final putt.

Baby, I'm all over that flat-screen HD/surround-sound kind of life. That black and white, sorry excuse of an existence is outta here. My guess is, if you've read along this far with me, that's where your heart's desire is as well. You're craving the relationship God has offered to you, am I right?

Then let's do it. Let's take the plunge and learn how to get started.

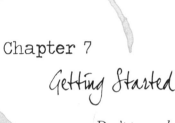

Chapter 7

Getting Started

> *Don't pray when you feel like it. Have an*
> *appointment with the Lord and keep it.*
> *A man is powerful on his knees.*
> —CORRIE TEN BOOM

A prayer life rich with meaning and significance doesn't just happen. So if you're expecting some kind of divine intervention into your oh-so-busy schedule, don't hold your breath. Planning ahead to set aside a specific time and place to meet with your heavenly Father is must-do if you're ever going to be consistent.

Morning Glory

You're probably not going to like this, but hear me out. I used to think it didn't matter what time of day you set aside to meet with the Lord so long as you do it. Now I know better. The later in the day, the more likely the interruptions and distractions. But what finally changed my thinking was this realization: Did I really want to give God the leftover crumbs of my day? He deserves the best. When might that be? Come on, now. Say it with me: In the morning. See? That wasn't so hard, was it?

I should probably fess up. I wasn't always a morning person. Not even close. That all changed a few years ago when I had to go back to work. As I mentioned in chapter 1, I hadn't worked outside the home for almost fifteen years. Just the thought of getting back into the everyday grind of a job was enough to make this grown woman freak. But I landed a good job (okay, my sister pulled some strings for me) and gradually eased back into the rat race.

The only drawback? I had to be there at six. In the morning. With a half-hour commute, I had to set my alarm for 4:30. In the morning. I always made it to work on time, but with each passing day it felt like I would get up, get dressed, and drive downtown on auto-pilot. Eight hours later, I'd drive home on auto-pilot (don't act so righteous—sometimes you do it too). By the time I got home and fed the family, I was beat.

I quickly learned that my brain was toast by seven in the evening. This was around the time I experienced my meltdown, which led to my challenge to God (see chapters 1 and 2). As part of that daring, scandalous ultimatum, I began setting my alarm for 3:45 in the morning. That allowed me ample time to get dressed, have an early breakfast (coffeecoffeecoffeecoffee), then spend a minimum of half an hour with the Lord each morning. I won't lie—it was hard at first. Never had I hated anything as much as the sound of that blasted alarm clock. But I was also desperate. I knew that in order to keep my half of the bargain to meet with Him each morning, I had no choice but to drag my sleepy carcass out of the sack.

With each passing day, then each passing week, it got easier. I'd established a routine that I slowly, slowly began to cherish. You have no idea what a monumental change of attitude that was for me. In the quiet of the morning, long before the sun came up or anyone else in the family awoke, I had the privilege of unhurried, uninterrupted time with my Lord and Savior.

Someone once said that God waits patiently for us, longing to spend time with us. I'm a very visual person. Tell me something and I'll forget it in five seconds. Show me something and it sticks. When I read a novel, I actually see the story played out like a movie in my head. When I set goals, I have to see the end result by picturing what it might look like. So when I began to think about these morning appointments with God, a very specific visualization popped into my head. Stay with me, now. This will probably sound a bit daft, but I have a point.

In my mind, I saw myself coming downstairs and finding Jesus waiting for me there in the family room off to the right at the bottom of the stairs. (Not that my house has a family room at the bottom of the stairs. In fact, to be honest, it actually looked more like Ward Cleaver's study in *Leave It to Beaver*. And for the record, it scares me to think that you might not even know who Ward Cleaver is. I warned you this was weird.) But in this particular imaginary room, two loveseats face each other in the middle of the room with a coffee table between them. Jesus is sitting there, His legs stretched out, feet propped up with ankles crossed on the coffee table. He holds a steaming mug of coffee in His hands.

When I enter the room, He looks up with a warm, genuine smile that seems to say, "Diane! I'm so glad you're here. I was hoping we'd have some time together this morning." I take a seat across from Him and reach for the mug of coffee He offers me . . .

Don't get me wrong. I don't view that cup of coffee He's prepared for me as an expectation on my part that He's there to serve me. Rather, I see it as symbolic of His expectation that I'll be joining Him. He's prepared for our time together. This puts the ball in my court. Will I make time for Him? Or will I ignore His presence there, waiting for me?

Listen to what Ann Graham Lotz has to say on this matter of expectation.

> Have you ever considered that you have a divine appointment when you get up early for your quiet time of prayer and meditation on His Word? . . . That Jesus is patiently, personally waiting to meet with you there? . . . What a difference it would make in our attitude of expectancy and our habit of consistency if we truly wrapped our hearts around the knowledge that each is a divine appointment, that Jesus Himself is waiting to meet with us.[1]

As I sit across from Him, I'm so utterly grateful to find Him here, I'm almost speechless. Then we begin to talk. . . . I hang on His every word, warmed by the depth of His love and compassion for me. I'm filled with such awe and wonder, so bewildered that He has made time for me—for such a wretch like me—when I so rarely make time for Him. And I'm driven to my knees, asking His forgiveness. Eventually, He dries my tears, helps me back to my seat, then He asks—of all things—what's on my heart this morning.

I honestly have no earthly idea where that visual came from, but that's probably because it wasn't an earthly idea at all. Think about it. God made me. He wired me a certain way, giving me certain unique gifts and characteristics that combine to make me who I am—including this outrageous visually-oriented tendency. It only makes sense that He could have put this scene into my head as a way to court my heart back to Him. In other words, He gets me because He made me!

This visualization has had an amazing effect on me, always reminding me not to miss the blessing of our morning visits. If the day gets away from me, I picture myself flying down those stairs, rushing toward the front door. Then I catch a glimpse of Him still there in the family room, still waiting for me, and I ask myself if there's anything more important than spending a few moments with my Jesus. The answer is always the same: nothing. Nothing is more important.

I know what you're thinking. *Fine, Diane. Mornings work for you. That's great. But my mornings are impossible. Any attempt at prayer that early would be a waste of time. I just can't think clearly until much later in the day.* (I won't tell your boss. Your secret's safe with me.) I understand and I sympathize. And if you can tell me that your evening or bedtime prayer time works for you, that you genuinely experience God in those remaining moments of your day, then more power to you.

Want to hear something funny? After I left my job, I rarely set my alarm, and I continued to wake up long before dawn. I could never "sleep in" like I used to. It didn't matter what time I went to bed, I'd still wake up at four or five. For the longest time, it frustrated me, this inability to sleep until a normal hour. Then it hit me. My inner-alarm clock was helping me keep those early morning prayer times I'd learned to cherish. It was as if God was nudging me, helping me to stay faithful to our morning visits. What I had seen as a curse turned out to be a tremendous blessing.

Okay, fine! Enough with the morning campaign already! Sorry. I guess I'm like someone who quits smoking and becomes a No-Smoking Nazi around others who light up. But I'm convinced that morning is the optimal time for more than just a passing prayer. Here's a thought.

Do not have your concert first and tune your instruments afterward. Begin the day with God. Begin the day with the Word of God and prayer, and get first of all into harmony with Him.

—James Hudson Taylor[2]

What a great quote. It's even more meaningful when you learn about the man who said it. In the late nineteenth century, James Hudson Taylor became the first Christian missionary to the interior of China where he founded the China Inland Mission. He ministered there for more than fifty-one years and eventually set up more than 205 mission stations staffed with 849 missionaries. Thousands of Chinese came to know Christ as a direct result of his efforts there. His passion for the Chinese still serves as living proof of what God can do in our world if only we'll open our hearts and lives to be used by Him.

Still not convinced about this whole morning thing? Don't take my word for it. Take a look at a few verses from the Bible (italics mine).

Morning by morning, O LORD, you hear my voice;
> morning by morning I lay my requests before you
> and wait in expectation.

—Psalm 5:3

But I will sing of your strength,
> *in the morning* I will sing of your love;
for you are my fortress,
> my refuge in times of trouble.

—Psalm 59:16

But I cry to you for help, O LORD;
> *in the morning* my prayer comes before you.

—Psalm 88:13

Satisfy us *in the morning* with your unfailing love,
   that we may sing for joy and be glad all our days.
                              —Psalm 90:14

I rise *before dawn* and cry for help;
   I have put my hope in your word.
                              —Psalm 119:147

I've stated my case. I've even thrown in the big guns of scripture. But in the end, the decision is up to you. No matter when you do it, just do it.

A Quiet Place

Now that we've settled that, let's talk about where to have your prayer time. When you think about meeting God for a time of prayer, what does that look like to you? (If you're tempted to use Ward Cleaver's study, I'm sorry but it's already occupied.) Is there a specific room or area that invites you in?

More than any other consideration, you need to find a place with the least amount of distractions. If the bed feels too conducive to sleep, you need to go elsewhere. If the kitchen table in your home rivals Times Square on New Year's Eve, you might want to scratch it off your list. If the TV in your family room proves to be too tempting, then flee its unholy clutches! Run, baby, run!

I'm ashamed to tell you this, but in the spirit of full disclosure to encourage you by my many, many blunders, I shall. Even after I got into the practice of my early morning prayer times, I still had—and still have—a lot to learn. During the winter months of the year, when it's too cold to sit out on my back porch, I curl up on our sofa in the family room. I normally have my coffee and breakfast first in an attempt to be fully awake and cognizant before attempting to pray. I figured God wasn't too thrilled with me nodding off all the time. What better way to get cognizant than to watch the news while munching on my granola, right? Problem is, I'd get sucked in by the teasers of upcoming news stories. Teasers by their very nature are intended to string you along and keep you watching.

So I'd pour another cup of coffee, put the news on mute, go ahead and open my prayer journal, and start praying. Yeah. Like that honors God. I don't know who I thought I was fooling by keeping one eye on the TV and the other on my journal, but there it is. The true, uncensored confessions of a prayer slacker. Eventually I came to my senses, set up a specific time frame, and turned off the TV before praying. See? I'm maturing. Really. I am.

More than likely I wouldn't have shared that embarrassing morsel of failure except that I'm sure that you, my friend, have also had some crazy prayer adventures of your own. Like trying to pray while you drive to work with the radio on. Syndicated radio talk show hosts Rick and Bubba are a scream and completely open about their faith in Christ, but they don't demand your undivided attention like God does, now do they?

Seriously, stop and think about where to meet with your Father. Whether it's an easy chair by the fireplace, a comfortable nook in your bedroom, or a patio table out on the deck, make it yours. Make it special so that each time you pass by, you're reminded that *this* is where you meet with God.

My sister heard about a suggestion to set aside a special chair for God when you meet with Him. She used to have her morning prayer time in a leather armchair in her guest bedroom. Now she sits on the bed, leaving that leather chair empty to remind her that she's there to meet with her Lord and Savior. She told me how much more personal and meaningful her prayer times have become as she thinks of Him sitting there before her. Interesting idea, don't you think?

After graduation from seminary, my husband was called to serve as minister of youth and education on a church staff in Naples, Florida. We loved our pastor, Max Cadenhead, and Ken felt blessed and honored to serve with him. One Saturday night after returning to the church from a youth outing, we noticed the lights on in the sanctuary. We opened a back door and saw Max up on the platform, lying prostrate on his face, praying passionately to the Lord. We quietly closed the door, not wishing to intrude on his privacy; but we were overwhelmed with appreciation for this humble man of God. We later learned he spent time every Saturday night there in the sanctuary, praying for the message God had given him for Sunday and for those who would hear it. He wasn't performing before an audience. He was on his face before God, seeking God's wisdom in preparation for Sunday's services.

I'm not suggesting you sneak into your church on Saturday night to pray on the platform. And by all means, leave me out of it should you do so and get arrested. What I am suggesting is for you to put some serious thought into where you will have your daily, divine appointment with God.

We've talked about the best time to pray. We've looked at options for where to pray. In our next chapter, how about we take a look at what you might need to make the most of your time with God?

Chapter 8
Gotta Haves

*The seeds of great discoveries are constantly
floating around us, but they only take root
in minds well prepared to receive them.*
—JOSEPH HENRY

Yⁱou've set a time. You've picked out your own special place.
You're almost ready. Only one more suggestion before
you get started: Come prepared and equipped.

I know what you're thinking. *Who needs "stuff" to pray?
Why can't I just pray?* Ah. Glad you asked. Obviously, you can
pray anytime and anywhere the urge hits you. But we're focused
here on your set-aside, one-on-one daily visit with God. To
make the most of the time you've allotted, you need to consider
including the following.

A Bible

I usually read at least one chapter a day, working my way
through different books of the Bible. If it's a long chapter, I'll
break it down and read it over the course of several days. The
point isn't how much scripture you read, but that you're
reading it. The psalms are a perfect launching pad, and

there are thousands of great verses throughout its 150 chapters. I switch back and forth between Old and New Testament books. If you've never read the Bible through, that's always a great way to learn about the Bible. Your local Christian bookstore has all kinds of planners to help you do that. Starting in Genesis isn't necessarily the best way, so don't hesitate to get some help. We'll talk more about this in chapter 10.

A Prayer Journal

I've never found the perfect journal for praying. And believe me, I've looked. Either they have only blank pages in a bound book, or they come filled with things I don't really use or need. When I first started journaling, I used those blank journals with exotic, enticing covers. But I quickly realized a bound book was too confining. I needed a loose-leaf notebook so that I could add or pull pages from one section to another.

One of these days I'd like to design a prayer journal. If you've got unlimited monetary resources and you're looking for a worthy investment, call me. I'll bring my prototype. We'll do lunch. For now I've made do by converting a Day-Timer® notebook for my needs. You can find them at most office supply stores. Mine is one of the smaller Day-Timers®, approximately 5x7 inches, with a cover that zips. These usually come with colorful tabbed dividers, a calendar, notepads, and lots of other accessories.

By the way, that notepad is essential. Trust me on this. It never fails—I start praying and BAM! I'll think of something I need to pick up at the store or a phone call I need to remember to make. At my age, if I don't write it down, it is gone. Now, instead of having to go dig through my kitchen drawer for a scrap of paper, I just flip over to the notepad in my Day-Timer® journal and make a note to myself. Same thing for the calendar that comes with the Day-Timer®. It's amazing how often, in the middle of my prayer time, my mind will begin to wander . . . *Is my dental appointment this week or next?* Or *Which day is the dog scheduled for her grooming?* But rather than get distracted, I just turn to the calendar, check on it, then immediately get back to praying.

I sincerely believe these rabbit-chases—dog, dental, or otherwise—are nothing more than attempts by the devil to yank us out of our time alone with God. Which only proves how important it is to be prepared for his fiery darts . . . which reminds me of a pastor whose tongue got tangled when he used that expression. I'll let you figure out what he said. An innocent blunder, but I still chuckle every time I hear the term.

The most effective prayer journal is the one you can best adapt to suit your own individual needs. Once you get into this daily habit, you'll know exactly what kind of journal works best for you. How is my prayer journal set up? I thought you'd never ask.

In the first section of my journal, I have my "Thank God" entries. Every morning, I start out my prayer time by writing down at least one thing I'm thankful for. A cool breeze on a summer's day. A letter from a good friend. A warm bed to sleep in on a cold winter's night. The brilliant splash of color in my flower garden. I find it helps put me into a prayerful attitude of gratitude and praise. It helps me focus on my God and Father.

Then I take the opportunity to come clean before God and ask for His forgiveness: a confession session, if you will. It's important to get rid of anything that might stand between you and God in this time you have together. But the following words might not be the best way to start off that prayer.

Dear Lord,

So far today, I'm doing all right. I have not gossiped, lost my temper, been greedy, grumpy, nasty, selfish, or self-indulgent. I have not whined, complained, cursed, or eaten any chocolate. I have charged nothing to my credit card. However, I will be getting out of bed in a few minutes, and I will need a lot more help after that. Amen.

Silly, I know, but haven't we all had days like that? Better yet, here's a great verse to help get your heart and your mind prepared.

Search me, O God, and know my heart;
Try me and know my anxieties;
And see if there is any wicked way in me,
And lead me in the way everlasting.
—Psalm 139:23-24, NKJV

I used to just pray, "God, forgive me for anything in my life that's not pleasing to You." I eventually realized that was nothing more than a quick bypass, avoiding any serious confession of specific problem areas in my life. Now, in this section of my prayer journal, I have a list I run through to help "search me, O God, and know my heart." It includes a search of:

- my thoughts
- my actions
- my words
- my attitudes
- things I've neglected to do
- times I've ignored God's prompting
- times I've yanked back control in certain areas of my life

It's by no means a conclusive list, but it's a start. I find it much more revealing of what's really happening in my heart. I also make a special effort to once again visualize Jesus sitting across from me, hearing my prayers. If I'm talking to Him face-to-face, I want to make sure there's nothing standing between us. And remember, as the French proverb says, "There is no pillow so soft as a clear conscience." Can I hear an amen to that?

The next section is for intercessory prayers; prayers for others. It is so important to have written records of these prayers, enabling you to trace God's hand through all the answers He provides. Again, you'll know best how to set up this section for your own needs. In my journal, members of my family, extended family, and close friends each have their own page. Over time, as these pages accumulate I'll paper-clip them together. I never toss any of these previous pages because it records a history of prayer for that individual. I also have a page for my church, its staff members and families, as well as church family prayer requests.

I also have a page for urgent/special prayers for world or national tragedies—hurricanes or other violent weather, fatal accidents, wars, etc. When you actually see a written record chronicling the growing number of missing and murdered children, or the heartbreaking occurrences of missing and murdered wives, particularly pregnant wives killed by their husbands, you tend to pray at a much deeper level for those involved and for their families.

In this section I keep other pages like "Prayers for America," including daily prayer for our president and the leaders of our country. There's also a list of those I'm praying for who need to come to a saving faith in Jesus Christ. What a joy to see an answer to these prayers, some after decades of praying.

The last section is for my personal prayers. It's amazing how these journal entries begin to tell the story of your prayer life. It helps pinpoint areas of your life that need special attention and enables you to see some of the amazing ways that God has guided you and led you. It also helps you recognize recurring problems, challenging you to figure out why you keep dealing with the same issues over and over.

Again, it's up to you how your journal is set up. Remember, I'm not the boss of you! It is, after all, just between you and God.

Devotionals*

Why the asterisk, you ask? I tend to think of devotionals, books and prayer guides as optional. I've used them from time to time—some I've read over and over. If you have the time and the desire to add this to your prayer time, that's great. As long as it isn't sidetracking you from actually praying.

The ACTS Formula

I usually avoid things that come across as gimmicky. I can smell 'em a mile away. Why is it so many Christians cling to over-the-top schemes or methods to accomplish their purposes? I'm actually quite persnickety about these practices. Such as preachers who always use alliteration for key points in their sermons. It's bad enough when it's the first letter of the words, but the ones that set my teeth on edge are those that alliterate an entire phrase.

1. Suffer in silence to serve the Lord.
2. Sacrifice in solitude to save the lost.
3. Surrender in surgery to sweeten the leotards.

Okay, skip that last one. You get my drift. I always get the feeling these guys sit around for hours, cramming their sermon topics into these icky little devices. Give us a break, brother. And then there's the old-school favorite, "Pack-a-Pew Night." Church members are assigned a row of pews and are expected to fill it with friends, family, and other acquaintances. The winner with the most guests gets the coveted bragging rights and/or first in line at the ice cream social following services. Because everyone knows Christians love to eat, amen? If these practices come across cheesy to you and me, we can only imagine how corny they appear to non-believers.

But while these tricks of the trade grate on my nerves, I have to say there's one that can help structure your prayer time. It's not really a gimmick (I just wanted an excuse to dish out some of my Christianese pet peeves!). It's more of a tool. It's an acronym to help organize your prayers by reminding us of the order in which to pray: **ACTS**.

Adoration: giving glory to God for who He is.
Confession: asking forgiveness for our sins.
Thanksgiving: expressing appreciation for the
    many things He has done for us.
Supplication: praying for needs in our own lives
    and those of others.

You have to admit, it's a great guideline. Instead of starting our prayer time with a long list of gimmes, it helps us to first recognize God and praise Him for His many attributes. Then, as I mentioned before, it's important to come clean with the Lord, asking His forgiveness for those areas in our lives that aren't pleasing to Him; for wrongs we've committed, both in action, in word, and in thought; and for the sins of omission, when we've neglected what we know is right. Next, to give thanks for all that He has blessed us with, for all the things He's doing in our lives and the lives of others. Finally, then, we can petition our Father for specific needs.

So there you have it. You're armed and ready to roll. We've discussed the whys, the wheres, and the how-tos. But there's so much more to think about as you start on this incredible journey. Take a break if you must, but please don't stop here.

Chapter 9

Getting to Know Your God

We look upon prayer simply as a means of getting things for ourselves, but the biblical purpose of prayer is that we may get to know God Himself.
—OSWALD CHAMBERS[1]

There's a unique dance of sorts that occurs between new friends. (For my traditional Baptist readers, be advised the use of "dance" here is a figure of speech, so just calm down.) In this dance, you're finding out what you have in common, picking up subtle hints about likes and dislikes, and in general, paving the way for this newfound relationship. But if you're like me, not all of your friendships are on an even keel. That pavement may be seriously lopsided by those friends who tend to dominate the relationship. One talks more, one has more crises, one is more demanding—any of this sounding familiar?

Picture this: You have a friend. You spend a lot of time with this friend whenever she's in town. You talk on the phone several times a week. You do lunch together when you can. But when I ask you to tell me about your friend, mostly you tell me about the hours you've spent on the phone with her or the many lunches or dinners you've shared.

"What are her hobbies?" I ask.

You pause. "You know, I'm not really sure."

"What are her passions?" I ask.

You pause again. "That's a good question. I'm not sure."

"Well," I begin, "what do you know about her?"

You tilt your head and look away, as if deep in thought. "Come to think of it, the only thing I do know is that she likes to hang out with me. And she lets me do most of the talking. I guess you could say she's a good listener. You might have noticed I like to talk a lot!" You laugh, amused at your own wittiness. Then you get that look of understanding in your eyes. "I've always thought of her as one of my best friends, but I guess it's a rather one-sided friendship. Strange, huh?"

"Definitely strange. And a bit sad, don't you think?"

"Yes. Maybe even pathetic."

Is that a tear I see in your eye?

"Well surely you can tell me her name, right?"

When you tell me her name, I recognize it immediately because she's one of my best friends! I begin to tell you about her beautiful oil paintings, many depicting scenes of her world travels.

"She paints? She's traveled the world?" you marvel. "I wondered why she was out of town so much, but I guess I never thought to ask."

I continue, telling you about her volunteer work at the children's hospital and the many children's books she's written and illustrated.

"You're kidding, right?" you ask. I detect a note of cynicism.

"And I'm guessing you probably don't know that she's also a pilot. She flies supplies to missionaries in Central America twice a year. You should hear some of her stories!" I say, looking off as I remember a tale about a mongoose on a Dominican runway . . .

"I wonder why she never told me those things?"

I study your expression. "Well, did you ever ask?"

You tilt your head again, squinting your eyes as you search your memory. "Uh . . . well, that's odd. I don't ever remember asking her much of anything."

I stare at you. "You should really get to know her. She's the most interesting person I've ever known."

You look at your watch. "Yikes! I'm late for my pedicure. Good to see you again, Sherry!"

As you rush away down the sidewalk, I drop my head with a heavy sigh. "Sarah. My name is Sarah."

Very funny, right? Not really. I actually know people like that. You probably do too. But let's put this discussion in a spiritual realm. If you've given your heart to God, trusting in His son Jesus Christ as your Savior, then you have a relationship with Him. We've already talked about how much He desires a personal relationship with you. But as Dr. Phil often asks, "How's that workin' out for ya?"

In all fairness, it's a little awkward, this relationship—what with you being human and Him being God of the Universe. At first blush, it's intimidating. Really, really intimidating. Granted, we can never know all there is to know about God because our little human brains and hearts cannot fully comprehend at that level of understanding. But don't let that stop you from getting to know Him as best you can.

Roll your sleeves up and put some effort into this, okay? Besides, I've got a wonderful secret that will help get you started.

The Names of God

Years ago I did a study on the names of God. I wasn't sure why I needed to learn about these specific names. I think I was mostly curious. I figured as long as I called Him God, Lord, or Father, and called His son Jesus, Christ, or Savior, I had all my bases covered. But I kept hearing people using those other names, so I decided to look into the subject and check it out.

One of the books I studied was *Lord, I Want to Know You* by Kay Arthur of Precept Ministries. Listen to why Kay Arthur suggests studying the names of God.

> In biblical times, a name represented a person's character. God's name represents His character, His attributes, His nature. To know His name is to know Him. To boast in His name is to have confidence in who He is![2]

Wow. Who knew that studying these Greek and Hebrew names of God could reveal so much more about the character of God?! It was like getting to know Him at a much deeper level than I ever imagined. The list below is by no means complete, but I want to share a few of these special names with you. My heart's desire is for these to spark a yearning in your soul to get to know God better and, by doing so, have a more personal prayer life with Him.

EL SHADDAI—Lord God Almighty; The God Who Is Sufficient for the Needs of His People

I will forever hear Amy Grant's version of the song "El Shaddai" whenever I read or hear this particular name of God.

El Shaddai. My all-sufficient God who is able to handle all my needs. Everything I will ever need I can find in Him. Think about that for a moment. Do you sense the power He offers us in those words? There is nothing, absolutely nothing in your life that He cannot handle. I wonder if it's possible for us to ever fully grasp the complete stress-free life He makes available to us when He promises, "My grace is sufficient for you" (2 Corinthians 12:9). Stop and think about that for a moment. What would that look like in your life? And how would it affect your prayer life?

ABBA—Father

I don't want to be the one to break it to you, but the original meaning of the word "Abba" didn't just pop up in the 1970s with the Swedish singing group. In fact, to be precise, the singers came up with their group's name by creating an acronym representing their four given names. So for now, my little dancing queen, put away your *Mamma Mia* CD and tune in to the one true Abba that offers so much more.

There is no more intimate name for God than *Abba*. The Aramaic word actually means "father," and in some cultures the meaning is even more closely akin to "Daddy." It's a name that's both heartfelt and warm and filled with respect. Just hours before His death, Jesus called out to His Father in prayer, "Abba Father, everything is possible for You. Take this cup from Me. Yet not what I will, but what You will" (Mark 14:36). We can call upon our Abba Father just as Jesus did, knowing the heart of the Father hears our every prayer.

EL ELYON—The Most High God

Sovereign and supreme, our Most High God is above all and over all. That pretty much covers everything, doesn't it? Seriously, if all we knew of God was this one name and the incredible magnitude of its meaning, we would never again know the meaning of worry. By understanding God's sovereignty—His absolute control over everything—we can live our lives in the utter security of trusting Him. It means we recognize the fact that nothing can happen to us without His permission. Look at what Colossians 1:16-17 has to say on this attribute of God's character.

> For by him all things were created: things in heaven and on earth, visible and invisible, whether thrones or powers or rulers or authorities; all things were created by him and for him. He is before all things, and in him all things hold together.

What is it you worry about most? What are the things that sometimes grip your soul and render you all but useless because you can't let go of them? By calling on El Elyon, you can begin to trust the One who knows far better how to deal with your yesterdays, your todays, and all your tomorrows. Such absolute confidence can add a whole new dimension to your prayer life as you come before El Elyon, your Most High God.

JEHOVAH—Self-Existent One: I AM WHO I AM

Most of us are familiar with the name Jehovah, probably because it's the name used for God more than any other—more than 6800 times in the Old Testament alone. Remember the story of the burning bush? Quite an attention getter there, that burning bush . . . In the midst of it, God explained to Moses that He had heard the cry of His people and was going to deliver them out of the hands of the Egyptians and bring them into the Promised Land. He instructed Moses to go before Pharaoh to plead on behalf of his people. But Moses was a wee bit hesitant, as you might imagine. Can't you just see him hold up his hands, "Who, me? Are you kidding?!"

Then Moses asked what to tell his people about all this if they should ask who sent him. Here's the Lord's response.

> God said to Moses, "I am who I am. . . . Say to the Israelites, 'The LORD, the God of your fathers—the God of Abraham, the God of Isaac and the God of Jacob—has sent me to you.' This is my name forever, the name by which I am to be remembered from generation to generation."
>
> —Exodus 3:14-15

The name Jehovah, or *Yahweh,* means self-existing. He was never created, has always been, and will forever remain. The Alpha and the Omega. When all around us life in this old world makes no sense, we have the everlasting promises of our Jehovah. We can come boldly before our Jehovah God in prayer because of those promises!

ELOHIM—The Creator

El means strength and unlimited power—two characteristics definitely required for the One who would speak all of life into existence. But what's especially interesting is the fact this Hebrew name for God is actually plural, designated by the —*him* ending, which implies three or more. Isn't that cool? So when the first verse in the Bible, Genesis 1:1, uses this word, it more literally means "In the beginning Three-in-one-God created the heavens and the earth"—referring to God the Father, God the Son, and God the Holy Spirit. Meaning, on page one of God's word He tells us exactly who He is!

> "You are worthy, our Lord and God, to receive glory and honor and power, for you created all things, and by your will they were created and have their being."
> —Revelation 4:11

All creation originated in Him. And unlike those who believe life began amidst some big bang or explosion, somehow just falling perfectly into place, we know that our Elohim had a plan and purpose for everything He created. That includes you and me. What is His purpose for you and me? We were created for Him. Each of us was given unique talents and interests and abilities, all for the purpose of glorifying God.

So tell me, how does such knowledge affect the way you'll pray to Elohim, your Creator?

Jehovah-Rapha—The Lord Our Healer

"He heals the brokenhearted and binds up their wounds" (Psalm 147:3). I love this verse. I've prayed it over and over for those who are hurting, those suffering a debilitating depression or physical trauma, and even for myself in times of need. God can heal the spirit, mind, and body. He's also keenly aware of the sin that corrupts our world, and He makes the following promise.

> If my people, who are called by my name, will humble themselves and pray and seek my face and turn

from their wicked ways, then will I hear from heaven
and will forgive their sin and will heal their land.

—2 Chronicles 7:14

The subject of healing is often difficult for us as humans
to wrap our minds around. Why is one healed and another
not? If God is all powerful as Jehovah-Rapha, then He is able
to heal everyone. So why doesn't He? This side of heaven, we
will never know the answers to such questions. Still, because
He loves us so much, we know we can trust Him—even with
our inability to understand or comprehend His ways.

Jehovah-shammah—The Lord Is There

He is everywhere. He is omniscient and omnipresent. He
knows everything far beyond our human capacity to know.
After Moses died, God called upon Joshua to lead His people
into the Promised Land. Now, as they were about to cross the
Jordan River, God promised to protect them with His presence.

No one will be able to stand up against you all the
days of your life. As I was with Moses, so I will be
with you; I will never leave you or forsake you.

—Joshua 1:5

For you and me, just knowing His presence is all around
us can help lift us from the darkest night, embrace us in the
loneliest hour, give us strength when we are tempted, and
enable us to live confident and secure in His promises.

Where can I go from your Spirit? Where can I flee
from your presence? If I go up to the heavens, you are
there; if I make my bed in the depths, you are there.

> If I rise on the wings of the dawn, if I settle on the far
> side of the sea, even there your hand will guide me,
> your right hand will hold me fast.
>
> —Psalm 139:7-10

ADONAI—Lord and Master

This name of God indicates a relationship. If He is indeed my Lord and Master, that means I must submit to Him in every area of my life. These days we cringe when we hear the word *submission*. We associate it with giving in and being weak. But by getting to know who He is, by digging into His Word and spending time with Him, we quickly learn that He is more than worthy of being our Lord and Master. If you knew without question that He would care for your every need, fight for you, protect you, and cherish you, would you hesitate to give yourself completely to Him? To submit to His lordship with your heart, soul, and body? Well, then, good news! The Bible is packed with promises that He'll do just that!

But once again, let me remind you that His being Lord is less about your needs being cared for and entirely about Him being worshipped and honored. It's the relationship. I bow to Him because He is My Lord and Master.

JEHOVAH-JIREH—The Lord Will Provide

One of the most heart-wrenching stories in the Bible is found in Genesis 22. God tells Abraham to take his only son, Isaac, to offer him as a burnt offering. I don't know about you, but I'm quite certain that I wouldn't have been able to follow the Lord's request to sacrifice one of my children. Yet the scripture tells us that Abraham did as he was told, following God's instructions even up to the point where he bound Isaac, laid him on top of the wood on the altar, then raised the knife to slay him.

Try to visualize Isaac's reaction: the wild fear in his eyes as he searches his father's face for some semblance of under-standing, the brokenhearted sadness he surely found there in his father's countenance. I cannot fully grasp the depth of this scenario no matter how many times I read it and regardless of the fact that I know how the story ends! I always hold my breath at this point in the story, with Abraham's arms stretched above him, his hands firmly grasping his knife, ready to take his son's life . . . until the Lord cries out, "Abraham! Abraham!" and rescinds His command.

Abraham has proven worthy, willing to sacrifice his only son for God. In return, God provided a ram for him to sacrifice in place of Isaac. Can't you feel the overwhelming relief that must have washed over him?! Don't you wonder how Isaac felt about this "test" between God and his father? Whoa. Just think about that for a moment.

Perhaps like you, I've heard and read this story many, many times in my life. Yet it still gives me goose bumps. But I also see the unforgettable, visual portrayal of God's love for us as it parallels the son He gave up on our behalf. Jesus was the sacrificial lamb who died to save us! And He did so willingly: "Not my will, but yours be done" (Luke 22:42).

Jehovah-Jireh, the Lord Will Provide. To me, this is the name that reveals more than any other the depth of God's love for us. But God not only makes provision for our salva-tion, He also provides for all of our needs. He sees our needs, He knows them even before we do, and He wants us to call upon Him for each and every one of them. Philippians 4:19

says, "My God shall supply all your need according to His riches in glory in Christ Jesus" (NKJV).

I'm not sure what it says about me (don't analyze me, bro), but this is one of my favorite names of God. Whether I'm praying for others or for a need in my own life, I call upon Jehovah-Jireh. What a privilege to know He's the one who extended the invitation to me to come to Him for my every need. What amazing grace!

More Names of God

I hope by now you've caught a glimpse of the astounding characteristics of God through the study of His names. There are many more, of course, and I invite you to make a personal commitment to study these further. Here are a few more to whet your appetite.

> *El Roi*—The God Who Sees
> *El Olam*—The Everlasting God
> *Jehovah-Shalom*—The Lord Our Peace
> *Jehovah-Sabaoth*—The Lord of Hosts
> *Jehovah-Raah*—The Lord My Shepherd
> *Jehovah-Nissi*—The Lord My Banner
> *Jehovah-Mekoddishkem*—The Lord Who Sanctifies You

So go ahead. Treat yourself! Spend some time getting to know your Lord God Jehovah, your Abba Father, your El Shaddai, your Adonai.

Chapter 10
God's Love Letter to You

To get the full flavor of an herb, it must be pressed between the fingers, so it is the same with the Scriptures; the more familiar they become, the more they reveal their hidden treasures and yield their indescribable riches.
—JOHN CHRYSOSTOM, A.D. 347-407

My pastor once said, "More than anything else, God breathed life into you so you could know Him." Yet most of us have no clue what it means to actually "know God." In the last chapter we studied some of the names of God, which helped give us a glimpse of who God is. But stopping there would be like the hockey player who suits up for games without ever going to practice. He may know how to skate, but he has no idea about the offensive and defensive strategies of the game. When he's blindsided by an opposing team member who smashes him against the wall, he slowly gets up, bruised and battered, and hurries off the ice. He may even rush out of the arena vowing never again to set foot on ice. He decides hockey should be played only by gifted athletes like Wayne Gretzky.

With righteous indignation, we scoff, "What a moron!" But just a minute. Are his actions any different from ours when it comes to studying the Bible? We may think it's all well and good for others, especially those "called" into ministry—pastors, preachers, and priests. It's their job, right? We shrug it off assuming we could never come close to understanding scripture, much less knowing God in that way. Better to leave that to the pros.

But what happens when you or I are blindsided like that hockey-player-wannabe? What do we do when life gets ugly and messy? How do we survive the shock of divorce or the death of a spouse or child or parent? How do we handle horrible physical injury from an accident? How do our soldiers and sailors move beyond life-changing battle wounds while serving in times of war?

Put yourself in any of those situations and tell me how you would handle such a tragedy. Until we've been there, we might like to think we'd cope. Somehow we'd make it. But when we're actually staring at the tiny coffin holding our baby's body, we realize "coping" isn't even in our vocabulary. Until we're comforting a son or husband who just lost both arms and legs when his convoy hit a roadside bomb, we have no idea how we'll ever make it another hour, day, or month—much less the rest of our lives.

The good news is we don't have to suffer alone. We don't have to carry the burdens of our messy lives alone. God is there for us. He wants to be the Comforter in Chief for the worst that life on this earth may hand us. But we need to know Him—genuinely know Him—not just when tragedy strikes. We need to know Him every moment of every day we live. We need to quit leaving it to the professionals and make knowing Him the most important mission of our lives.

Let me share a passage of scripture with you. The setting was the Lord's Supper. Jesus was giving His final words of wisdom and instruction to his disciples (and to us), knowing He would soon be arrested and crucified. Here's what He says.

> Abide in me, and I in you. As the branch cannot bear fruit by itself, unless it abides in the vine, neither can you, unless you abide in me. I am the vine; you are the branches. Whoever abides in me and I in him, he it is that bears much fruit, for apart from me you can do nothing. If anyone does not abide in me, he is thrown away like a branch and withers; and the branches are gathered, thrown into the fire, and burned.
>
> —John 15:4-6, ESV

We don't use the term *abide* much in our culture today. In the context of these verses, it represents the idea of being at home with or living with. Now don't get nervous or freaked out, but I actually looked up *abide* in the original Greek and discovered it's the word *meno*. It means "to stay (in a given place, state, relation, or expectancy): abide, continue, dwell, endure, be present, remain, stand."[1] In today's vernacular we might describe it as hanging out with someone on a personal level. I'm guessing Jesus knew we'd get confused about this whole concept, so He described it through the metaphor of a vine and its branches. If He is the vine and we are the branches, the only way we'll survive is for us to be connected to Him: to dwell with Him or to remain in a relationship with Him. Otherwise we shrivel up like those useless branches and get tossed in the fire.

You make the call: Abide with Jesus and get to know Him—or go your own way without Him and get toasted. Which will it be?

The Lord also gives us a beautiful promise in the next couple of verses of that passage.

If you abide in me, and my words abide in you, ask whatever you wish, and it will be done for you. By this my Father is glorified, that you bear much fruit and so prove to be my disciples. As the Father has loved me, so have I loved you. Abide in my love. If you keep my commandments, you will abide in my love, just as I have kept my Father's commandments and abide in his love. These things I have spoken to you, that my joy may be in you, and that your joy may be full.

—John 15:7-11, ESV

He just lays it all out there, doesn't He? He offers us the absolute purest form of joy if only we'll spend time with Him, live with Him, dwell in Him. Unfortunately, our selfish human tendency is to make a grab for the blessings He offers without any intention of actually doing the prerequisite abiding. *Gimme some of that vino, baby! Fill my glass to overflowing!* We completely blow it, ignoring the fact that the vineyard will only bear fruit if we take care of the vine.

"If you abide in me, and my words abide in you . . ."

The only way we will ever get to know God is by reading His Word. It's all there. He's written it all out for us. Everything we ever need to know about the God of the universe—the God who made you and me, the God who is able to provide every answer to every question we will ever have—is right there in the Bible.

Excuse me, did you just yawn while reading what I just said?

See, that's the problem. Most of us know little or nothing about the Bible. We've never spent any quality time reading it, let alone studying it. Oh, a snippet here, a verse there, but reading to study God's word? Hardly. Perhaps a few scripture verses attached to Sunday's sermon are outlined in our church bulletin. Great! But that was never intended to be the full extent of our Bible knowledge.

For those of us who may have grown up in church, attending Sunday school regularly, we may have an inkling about certain passages. We may have memorized the books of the Bible or participated in Bible drill contests. But we're sadly remiss if that was the last of our Bible training.

A side note, if I may. Yes, we're all responsible for our own lives and our individual walk with Christ. But I think a certain responsibility also falls on those who are called to preach and teach. For hundreds of years far too many men and women who have preached to us and taught us God's Word have taken the most important message in all of history and made it dry as sawdust. They've made the Living Word of Life so parched and tasteless it's a wonder anyone still listens.

When Ken was in seminary we attended a large metropolitan church in Fort Worth. We were part of dynamic Sunday school class of other young couples, most of them fellow seminary students. Our teacher was a vice president at the seminary. He was a phenomenal Bible teacher, and we loved both him and his precious wife.

The pastor of the church? Oh my. Let's just say we all had a nickname for him—Snooze Robbins (not his real last name; I'm not that heartless!). Honestly, it was an Olympic event just trying to stay awake during his messages. He was a beloved man who dearly loved the Lord, but he was long, long overdue for retirement. Somewhere along the line he just lost what I call that fire in the belly for preaching. I don't for a minute doubt his passion or heart for God. I think it was more a case of a worn-out delivery. Fortunately, while we were still there at seminary, he did in fact retire.

Then there are the overabundance of Bible teachers or preachers on television who drone on and on as if they're reading the phone book instead of God's love letter to us. Give me a break. Granted, I'm not a big fan of the screamers or the hell-fire-and-damnation preachers or those who sob through their messages. So I'm not sure which is worse. That's probably a matter of personal preference. But one thing I know: God's love letter to you and me is anything but bland!

Jim Davis was the minister of music at the downtown Tulsa church where I grew up. They broke the mold with Jim. He was out of the box before there was a box. The man was hilarious. We couldn't get enough of him, and those of us in the youth group often stopped by his office whenever we were at church. On the wall hung a framed poster of a traditional church service as seen from the preacher's point of view behind the pulpit. There on the first row is Jesus, dressed in biblical garb. He's slumped down in the pew, His legs stretched out in front of Him, crossed at the ankles, His head resting on the shoulder of the man next to Him. He's sound asleep. You can almost hear Him snoring. I love that poster. I can't tell you how many times I've thought of that poster through the years.

Dear pastor, if your preaching is that dull and boring, I beg you to take a sabbatical and try to find out why. What sucked the life out of your calling? How can you make the life-changing, astonishing good news of God's amazing love so monotonous and bland? What happened to your passion?

There's a wonderful verse in Psalm 34:8 where David cries out, "Oh, taste and see that the Lord is good!" Bland? Dull? Boring? No way.

Unfortunately, too many of us have never "tasted" to begin with; and for those who have, many were treated to a flavorless knock-off that was nothing like God intended. Please don't shun the greatest story ever told just because of some past "unsavory" experience.

Through the course of my life, I've attended a lot of different churches. From time to time I would hear murmurings in some of those congregations, something along the lines of, "I'm just not being fed spiritually here." I can't tell you how many times I've heard those exact words, no matter where I attended church. Such a strange concept to me. Whenever I heard it, I was always a little tempted to tie a bib around the person's neck and twist open a jar of baby food. It just seemed like the right thing to do.

It also struck me that the person making that statement was somehow implying he or she was just oh-so-much-more spiritual than the pastor of the church. Okay. I suppose that's entirely possible. But let's be honest. Is your spiritual health your pastor's responsibility, or is it yours? Because I've always thought of the whole church and Sunday message experience as so much icing on the cake. But it's my responsibility to make that cake! I'm responsible for my own spiritual growth, and so are you!

Isn't it time to yank off that bib and find out for yourself what's in this Love Letter God wrote you? Isn't it time you took your relationship with God to the next level and discovered all that it can be?

> Like newborn infants, long for the pure spiritual
> milk, that by it you may grow up into salvation—
> if indeed you have tasted that the Lord is good.
> —1 Peter 2:2-3, ESV

Spiritual milk is sufficient for spiritual "babes in Christ"; but as you grow, you require more. As the physical body needs protein, the spiritual body also yearns for something more substantial. We need to understand the teachings of Scripture, the depth of God's love, the call to tell others of God's grace, hope, and forgiveness. Sadly, many of us never grow beyond those babes in Christ. We're content to be spoon-fed; and if no one feeds us, we shrivel up spiritually and become useless. Envision grown adults still wearing diapers, if you will. They're everywhere. And yes, they're seated on the pews all around you. (I wonder if that's where the term "pew" came from? I'm aghast at the thought.)

In *Lord, Teach Me to Pray,* Kay Arthur put it this way: "If we do not know our God and His ways, our prayer lives will be impotent and ineffective."[2] And it all goes back to knowing God through His Word. Likewise, if we don't have a meaningful prayer life, we're never going to experience the life God intended for us to live. We may fool ourselves into thinking it's enough to attend church regularly or toss a few dollars into the offering plate, but we certainly don't fool God.

Do you have a serious hunger for God? A deep-seated yearning to know Him well enough that you're completely at ease in His presence as you pray? Then I challenge you to feed that hunger with some serious "meat" and satisfy that longing by dusting off your Bible and getting genuinely acquainted with Him, one-on-one.

Okay, I've made the commitment to start reading my Bible. But where do I start?

There are all manner of ways to study the Bible. The first order of business is picking out the right translation. Some would say the King James Version is the only accurate translation. Others find more updated translations—like the English Standard Bible or the New American Standard Bible—are easier to understand. Paraphrased versions are more reader-friendly but be advised they are just that—paraphrased. Stick to a good study Bible for more accurate translations.

Reading the Bible from start to finish—from Genesis to the book of Revelation—would never be a waste of time, but I don't think it's the best way to start. Do your homework. If your church offers a Bible study group, sign up for it. Check your nearest Christian bookstore for study books to help get you started. Find out which method appeals to you to get the most out of your reading. There are some excellent resources available to help you on this journey, like the Read-the-Bible-in-a-Year plans that offer a mix of Old and New Testament readings each day. That's a great way to get the overview of this magnificent book. Others suggest starting with the Gospels (Matthew, Mark, Luke, and John) in the New Testament—preferably starting first with the book of John, then reading through the rest of the New Testament. Whatever your choice, just make sure you have a plan and stick to it.

I'll never forget the first time my family attempted to have family Bible reading times together. I was probably eight or nine years old at the time. We'd recently moved to another state and joined a Bible-teaching church where families were encouraged to read the Bible together. After dinner one night, we all sat down in our living room. My father began reading the first chapter of Matthew. If you're not familiar with that chapter, it's a long list of names tracing the genealogy of Christ, going all the way back to Abraham in the Old Testament. The King James Version uses the term *begat*, which basically means "produced" or "gave birth to." Take a look.

The book of the generation of Jesus Christ, the son of David, the son of Abraham. Abraham begat

Isaac; and Isaac begat Jacob; and Jacob begat Judas
and his brethren; And Judas begat Pharez and
Zerah of Tamar; and Pharez begat Hezron; and
Hezron begat Ram.

—Matthew 1:1-3, KJV

Begat, begat, begat. It continues like this for the entire
chapter. Fascinating reading, I suppose, if you're into that sort
of thing. So Dad thought we should just skip over all those
verses and move along. Mom thought we should include
them. They got into quite a "discussion" over it; and long story
short, that was the end of our family Bible readings. My sister
and I looked at each other in silent sibling-speak. *What was
that all about?*

I know what you're thinking. How silly to let something
so trivial keep you from a meaningful family experience.
You're exactly right. But my parents were in uncharted terri-
tory and really had no idea how to go about it. They needed a
plan. They needed to know the best way to read through a
massive book that's hundreds of pages long, covering sixty-six
individual books, without getting tripped up.

To a newbie, I would give a quick caution. It's important
to note that the books of the Bible were written thousands of
years ago, and some have been translated from what are called
the dead languages. Meaning, there will be some passages that
are difficult to understand. There are also historical, cultural,
and linguistic differences to keep in mind, as well as a whole
truckload of literary devices and types. All the more reason to
join a Bible study group where you can work through the passages that may stump you on first read.

Case in point. There's a story in the second chapter of the
book of John that tells of the occasion when Jesus performed

His first public miracle. The setting was a wedding in Cana in Galilee. Jesus' mother, Mary, was also a guest at the wedding. At some point during the wedding, the wine ran out. Skimpy host? Over-imbibing guests? Who knows. But for some reason, the Bible tells us Mary went to Jesus and said, "They have no more wine." Did she know He had a special "gift set" for this type of thing? Probably so. There's no telling what kind of mysterious antics young Jesus had dazzled her with through the years. But He'd never performed any of those miracles in public before. And evidently, He wasn't ready to go public that day because He responded to her by saying, "Woman, what does this have to do with me?" (John 2:4, ESV)

As a mother, I'm thinking Mary's eyes would have sparked with instant fury. She would have yanked her son by His ear and said, "What did you just say to me, young man? You do not talk to your mother like that! I raised you better than that! Do you have any idea what I've gone through for You? Do you?! The ridicule I endured in our town when I was carrying You? The ridiculous accommodations I had to put up with at your untimely arrival that night in Bethlehem? Here—wanna see the stretch marks?! " At which point, Jesus surely would've groveled, apologized profusely, then come up with a better way to express Himself. Right?

Not so fast. See, we jump to all kinds of conclusions if we just give a quick read to passages of scripture like this. For years I was indignant that Jesus would talk to His mother like that—until I finally put on my big girl pants and decided to do some research. Turns out the original Greek word He used for "woman" in this verse isn't nearly as disrespectful as it sounds in today's English. In fact, Jesus used the very same term when He lovingly addressed His mother for the last time from the cross. But His use of that word toward her at that wedding in Cana was most likely a term of endearment that also served to gently inform her that their relationship would now change. He wasn't five any more. He was thirty years old, which in that time period was ancient. And if Mary unknowingly prodded Him into performing this "public" miracle of turning water into wine, perhaps He used the opportunity to let her know He was now stepping into His role as the Son of God, no longer Mary's little boy.

All that to say, the Bible is packed full of fascinating stories and relevant information for our lives. And it is worthy of our time and hopefully our passion to study it and learn about it, to dig beyond the mere words on the page to gain a more complete understanding of this love letter from God.

I think the more you know about the Bible, the more you'll want to dig deeper into specific books of the Bible. I love reading Psalms. It was probably the first book of the Bible I studied. Sunday school teachers taught us if we let our Bibles fall open in the middle, we'd find the psalms. I read through those 150 chapters at least two or three times a year.

Each time I do, it's like getting reacquainted with old friends. I've underlined favorite passages and highlighted particular verses, jotting down the dates when they had significant meaning in my life's journey. I usually read through the New Testament at least once a year. There, I spend a little extra time in the book of James and Paul's letters to the Ephesians and the Philippians—some of my favorite books.

I have friends who are completely fascinated by Revelation, the last book of the Bible, which is filled with prophecy. In other words, the Bible is quite literally a book that has something for everyone. That said, you really should read through the entire Bible at some point in your spiritual journey. Otherwise, it's much too easy to take things out of context or jump to inaccurate conclusions. In other words, read the book!

Once you become acquainted with God's Word and the many lessons and stories in it, you begin to understand more about your heavenly Father, whom you've committed to follow. With each new morsel of truth, you learn better how to live your life. You can finally begin to abide in Him as He has called you to do.

"So then faith comes by hearing, and hearing by the word of God" (Romans 10:17, NKJV). With that promise, we can rest in the assurance that we're walking according to His plan for our lives. It is the greatest adventure you'll ever live, my friend. Don't miss the blessing.

Chapter 11

In Search of Your "Want-To"

As the deer pants for streams of water,
so my soul pants for you, O God.
My soul thirsts for God, for the living God.
—Psalm 42:1-2

Unless you've dozed through the last ten chapters, you've hopefully been inspired to take the next step in your relationship with God and get serious about your prayer life. Awesome! If that's the case, my work is done! Even if you're only thinking about it more than you ever have, it's a start. Baby steps, my friend. We've all got to start somewhere.

But I'm guessing you're probably still struggling with a number of issues. Like what to do when your "want-to" isn't cooperating. In Chapter 6 I asked you how badly you want it, this prayer relationship with God. But what do you do when you know you should make time for God, but no matter how hard you try, you just can't seem to want to enough to do something about it? What should you do?

Good question. The mere fact you acknowledge there's a problem with your want-to is a sign you're moving in the right direction. And for the record, you're not alone with this one. Listen to what Quaker theologian Richard Foster has to say on this subject.

> When we cannot pray, let God be our prayer. Nor should we be frightened by the hardness of our heart: prayer will soften it. We give even our lack of prayer to God.[1]

We're all guilty of getting caught up in the world we live in and demoting God to the back of the bus. Or, like Briana's character in chapter 6, we grant Jesus access into only certain parts of our lives, in no uncertain terms. So maybe the solution is to take the focus off the lack of motivation on your part and shoot some light on how much He loves you. Remember the song you learned as a child, "Jesus loves me, this I know. For the Bible tells me so." Let's put that little verse to the test and see just how much God loves you. Don't just rush through these. Make sure the truth of each verse reaches deep into your heart.

> I lift up my eyes to the hills—
>   where does my help come from?
> My help comes from the LORD,
>   the Maker of heaven and earth.
> He will not let your foot slip—
>   he who watches over you will not slumber.
>   —Psalm 121:1-3

> The Lord is near to the brokenhearted,
>   And saves those who are crushed in spirit.
>   —Psalm 34:18, NASB

> I have set the LORD continually before me;
>   Because He is at my right hand, I will not be shaken.
>   —Psalm 16:8, NASB

In my distress I called upon the Lord,
     And cried to my God for help;
He heard my voice out of His temple,
     And my cry for help before Him came into His ears.
                                        —Psalm 18:6, NASB

Well, look at you—all grown up and reading scripture! I knew you could do it! But stay with me for this next one. It's quite a bit longer but one of the most intensely personal scriptures you'll ever read. Psalm 139 is indeed a love letter. In it, the psalmist describes the depth of God's love. If ever you find yourself doubting His utter devotion and love for you, camp yourself right here and bask in the freshness of His affection for you.

O Lord, you have searched me
     and you know me.
You know when I sit and when I rise;
     you perceive my thoughts from afar.
You discern my going out and my lying down,
     you are familiar with all my ways.
Before a word is on my tongue
     you know it completely, O Lord.

You hem me in, behind and before;
     you have laid your hand upon me.
Such knowledge is too wonderful for me,
     too lofty for me to attain.

Where can I go from your Spirit?
     Where can I flee from your presence?
If I go up to the heavens, you are there;
     if I make my bed in the depths, you are there.
If I rise on the wings of the dawn,

if I settle on the far side of the sea,
even there your hand will guide me,
your right hand will hold me fast.

If I say, "Surely the darkness will hide me
and the light become night around me,"
even the darkness will not be dark to you;
the night will shine like the day,
for darkness is as light to you.

For you created my inmost being;
you knit me together in my mother's womb.
I praise you because I am fearfully and wonderfully made;
your works are wonderful,
I know that full well.
My frame was not hidden from you
when I was made in the secret place.
When I was woven together in the depths of the earth,
your eyes saw my unformed body.
All the days ordained for me
were written in your book
before one of them came to be.

How precious to me are your thoughts, O God!
How vast is the sum of them!
Were I to count them,
they would outnumber the grains of sand.
When I awake,
I am still with you.

—Psalm 139:1-18

Hold on. I want you to go back and read through this passage from Psalm 139 once again, this time asking yourself if you honestly comprehend and embrace every word offered there.

Do you get it? Are you beginning to understand how intimately God knows and loves you? Overwhelming, isn't it? But just in case there's still an inkling of doubt in your mind, jump over to the New Testament and read this next verse:

> For God so loved the world that he gave his one and only Son that whoever believes in him shall not perish but have eternal life.
>
> —John 3:16

If there were a Scripture Hall of Fame, this verse would be Numero Uno. Because God didn't just talk the talk, He quite literally walked the walk. He was not only willing to die for you, He did die for you through the sacrifice of His Son Jesus Christ. He loves you! Do you believe that? Do the words of this verse resonate somewhere inside you? Do you understand that "whoever believes" means if you had been the only one, He still would have died for you?

Hold that thought for just one moment. I want to share something I read today in a magazine article about University of Florida quarterback Tim Tebow. If you know anything about this extraordinarily talented young man—the only sophomore ever to win the Heisman Trophy—you know he's not only one of the greatest college football players of our time, he's also an outspoken follower of Christ who sees his athletic abilities as a gift from God specifically as an opportunity to tell others about Christ. And Tebow really walks that walk. On game days, he's well-known for writing scripture references on his eye-black (that black sticker or grease below the eyes that helps reduce glare). For the January 8, 2009, BCS National Championship game against OU, Tebow wore "John 3:16" beneath his eyes. Check this out.

Within 24 hours of the game, the reference was googled 93 million times. More than passing or rushing yards, this was a statistic Tebow savored. It meant he'd achieved his dream of deflecting his fame to his Savior.[2]

Tim Tebow gets it. He understands the message of John 3:16. He knows that if he was the only one, Christ still would have died for him. And he lives his life out loud giving God the glory every chance he gets.

What about you? Do you get it? Does John 3:16 resonate in your life as if it matters? You don't have to be a Heisman Trophy winner to accept the gift of life Christ is offering to you. But you sure ought to understand the sacrifice Christ made to give you that gift of eternal life.

Let's take it one step further. Romans 8:31*b* asks, "If God is for us, who can be against us?" Excellent question. But don't make a common misinterpretation here. This isn't about God joining your team; it's about you joining His. I always love to hear athletes like Tim Tebow give God the glory after a big win, be it the National Championship, the Super Bowl, the World Series, the Olympics, or any other sporting event. But I'm pretty sure there are probably many other individuals on the opposing teams who love God—and whom God loves—just as much. Contrary to popular belief, the Almighty doesn't have pennants hanging around heaven, showing His preference for the Florida Gators (hard to believe but true, Gator fans), the Tennessee Titans, Boston Red Sox, Orlando Magic, or whatever team you happen to be rooting for. (Although I must admit, I've often wondered if He's misplaced His Chicago Cubs pennant. Think maybe His goat ate it?)

Abraham Lincoln was once asked if he believed God was on the side of the Union soldiers during the Civil War. He answered, "I don't ask God to choose sides. I want to be on His side since He is always right." Preach it, Abe!

The point is, we need to leave our pride and our egos behind, because it's not about us. It's totally about Him. So often we barge ahead, making our decisions and following our plan of action, then ask Him to bless it, as if somehow He owes it to us. Then we're baffled when things get screwed up and don't turn out the way we want them to. If only we'd learn, as we talked about earlier, to stay out of that pilot's seat and let Him take control. Don't you wonder why He puts up with all the stupid mistakes we make over and over and over?

It's called grace. Unmerited favor from God. Hard for us to comprehend, but it's one of the biggest blessings He offers us.

Hey, I've got good news for you. Skip down to the last two verses of Romans 8 and see what else Paul has to say about God's love for us.

> For I am convinced that neither death nor life, neither angels nor demons, neither the present nor the future, nor any powers, neither height nor depth, nor any-thing else in all creation, will be able to separate us from the love of God that is in Christ Jesus our Lord.
> —Romans 8:38-39

None of those things will stand in the way of God's love for you! Got it? *He loves you!!!* Any questions? If not, let's move on.

Chapter 12
The Lord's Prayer 101

Pray then like this . . .
—MATTHEW 6:9A, ESV

We're having coffee, you and I. You know I'm writing a book about prayer, so I discern you want to ask me a question. Go for it. I'm all ears. You tell me that you often say the Lord's Prayer and even an occasional meal-time prayer of thanks. Then you ask, "Isn't that enough?"

Well, that depends. If you're satisfied to keep your relationship with God at arm's length, then you're good to go. But now it's my turn to ask you a question. When you pray the Lord's Prayer, do you dwell on the words you're saying? Are you cognizant of what you're actually praying? Or have you said the words so often that you rattle off the prayer without really thinking, like praying on autopilot?

Have you ever driven somewhere only to arrive at your destination without any conscious memory of the actual drive that got you there? This happens frequently for those who drive to and from work each day. Quite a shock when you pull into your parking place and haven't a clue where your mind was for the duration of your commute, isn't it?

When I was growing up in Tulsa, we made the drive from the suburbs to our downtown church so often that sometimes we'd get halfway there only to realize we meant to go somewhere else! It's a little frightening to think how many folks get behind the wheel of a car or truck only to check out mentally. We've all done it. It's a miracle any of us are still alive.

If we're honest, when we pray the same exact prayer every day without giving it so much as a single attentive thought, we're not really praying at all. We're merely reciting words memorized long ago that may or may not have *ever* held any significance because we've never opened our hearts and our minds to their meaning. How pathetic is that? And be assured God is not impressed. He knows our hearts. He knows whether we're plugged in or just stopping by for a quick tip of the hat in His direction. Matthew 6:7 (ESV) says, "And when you pray, do not heap up empty phrases as the Gentiles do, for they think that they will be heard for their many words."

Oh, dear. I'm afraid I have another confession to make. (If you're keeping count, don't. I might have to hurt you.) Despite my journey to learn all I can about having a meaningful prayer life, I have to admit there have been times I've merely gone through the motions. More often than I care to mention. I've always wondered how the mind can do two things at once. Like reading something only to realize your mind was actually somewhere else entirely. How is that even possible? Happens to me all the time. Especially when I'm reading the Bible. In my head, I can hear myself reading the words on the page. But it dawns on me minutes or pages later that I've been consumed with thinking about something else entirely. When the realization hits me, I'm embarrassed, knowing God isn't amused or impressed. Oh, I'm quite sure

He's used to it, and not just from *moi*. But once again, I'm on my knees asking His forgiveness.

Even as we pray, it's also very easy to slide into another bad habit: the mindless recitation of requests—God bless Susie, God bless Fred, God bless Debbie, God bless Ted . . . But let's be honest. If these prayers are nothing more than meaningless arrows shot heavenward, they don't exactly represent a heart that's deeply passionate about these people, do they? Who do we think we're fooling? I suppose these rote prayers are better than nothing, but they certainly won't enrich your relationship with God. Let's face it, if this is your idea of what prayer is all about, you might as well just jot down your list of concerns, then stuff it in your Bible, tell God where He can find it if He's interested, and let it go at that. Seriously, why bother?

John Bunyan once said, "In prayer it is better to have a heart without words than words without a heart." If it's the desire of your heart to grow in your walk with your Lord and Savior, then you understand prayer must be a purposeful matter of the heart.

When Jesus taught the multitudes how to pray, He prefaced His model prayer with a few warnings, including this one in Matthew 6:5 (ESV).

> And when you pray, you must not be like the hypocrites. For they love to stand and pray in the synagogues and at the street corners, that they may be seen by others.

Did you catch that? Jesus called them hypocrites. He wasn't fooled by these bragging fakers. Neither is He fooled by you or me today when we pray in any manner that's not sincere and heartfelt.

Speaking of the Lord's Prayer, it's important to remember that Jesus taught us this prayer for us to use it as a model. We seem to skip over the first four words in the introduction of this most famous of all prayers. Jesus said, "Pray then *like this*" (Matthew 6:9, ESV, emphasis added). He didn't say, "Pray this exact prayer, these exact words," did He? It's a guide or outline, if you will, in which He instructed us how to pray. You can be sure He never intended for us to merely recite these words in mindless repetition. Look at it as a template for your prayers.

To acknowledge God's presence.
> *Our Father in heaven,*
> *hallowed be your name.*

To proclaim God's sovereignty.
> *Your kingdom come,*
> *your will be done*
> *on earth as it is in heaven.*

To submit our needs before Him.
> *Give us this day our daily bread.*

To ask for forgiveness.
> *and forgive us our debts,*

To forgive others.
> *as we also have forgiven our debtors.*

To ask for God's protection.
> *And lead us not into temptation,*

To ask God to rescue us from the sin of the world.
> *but deliver us from evil.*

—Matthew 6:9-13, ESV

He gave us the perfect formula for prayer. But did you know He also hears your prayers even when the words don't form on your lips?

Likewise the Spirit also helps in our weaknesses. For we do not know what we should pray for as we ought, but the Spirit Himself makes intercession for us with groanings which cannot be uttered . . . He makes intercession for the saints according to the will of God.

—Romans 8:26-27, NKJV

To intercede means to plead on another's behalf. When we are worried or confused or so heartbroken that we can't find the words to pray, Paul reminds us that God's Holy Spirit will plead on our behalf. He expresses for us what we cannot. On the darkest night, He is there for us. Why? As I keep telling you, He loves you!

Chapter 13

When God Is Silent

Hear my prayer, O LORD,
Listen to my cry for help;
Be not deaf to my weeping.
—PSALM 39:12A

Whenever the subject of prayer comes up, people always want to talk about the prayers they prayed that God didn't answer. It always amazes me how ready these individuals are to dismiss the whole concept of prayer based on one single prayer that wasn't answered—at least not in their eyes. It's like the Pony Prayer we talked about previously: Prayed for a pony, didn't get the pony, therefore prayer is a waste of time. Hopefully we've made a little progress since that savory discussion. But just as a reminder, be assured that God always, always answers prayer. As we discussed earlier, He answers in one of three ways: yes, no, or not now. So if you think God hasn't answered your prayer, it's possible He just hasn't answered it yet. Don't believe me?

> Ask and it will be given to you; seek and you will find; knock and the door will be opened to you. For everyone who asks receives; he who seeks finds, and to him who knocks, the door will be opened.
> —Luke 11:9-10

That promise came straight from Jesus. No ifs, ands, or buts (okay, maybe a couple "ands"); He simply lays it out. The Greek translation of these verbs makes the promise even more compelling. Written in present tense, they are more accurately translated as *keep on asking, keep on seeking, and keep on knocking*. What does that tell you? Don't give up! Keep praying!

Look back a few verses. In Luke 11:5-8, Jesus tells a story to explain this concept.

> Then he said to them, "Suppose one of you has a friend, and he goes to him at midnight and says, 'Friend, lend me three loaves of bread, because a friend of mine on a journey has come to me, and I have nothing to set before him.'
>
> Then the one inside answers, 'Don't bother me. The door is already locked, and my children are with me in bed. I can't get up and give you anything.' I tell you, though he will not get up and give him the bread because he is his friend, yet because of the man's persistence he will get up and give him as much as he needs.

Get the visual here. It's midnight. Joe has unexpected company drop by. His fridge is empty, the cupboard is bare, so rather than wake Mrs. Joe (bless his heart), he rushes over to his neighbor's house and starts knocking on the door. Nick the Neighbor yells from inside (in a Yiddish accent, no doubt), "Go away! It's after midnight! They're your company, you feed them! For crying out loud, we're sleeping in here!" But Joe isn't deterred. Have you ever had someone hold their finger on your doorbell? Annoying, isn't it? That's our Joe. No one had doorbells in those days, but he just kept knocking and knocking, making all kinds of racket. Nick may shout a few expletives at him, but eventually he gets up and opens the door. "All right! All right! I'm up! Oy vey! Enough with the noise, already!" He probably never stopped the whining, but good Neighbor Nick goes into his kitchen and gives his friend and neighbor as much food as he needs.

You've gotta love the guy's persistence. And therein lies the lesson Jesus was trying to make. Keep on asking! Keep on seeking! Keep on knocking! Because God will answer your prayers. Every time? Always!

> Be joyful always, *pray continually*, give thanks in all circumstances, for this is God's will for you in Christ Jesus.
> —1 Thessalonians 5:16-18 (emphasis added)

Max Lucado is one of the best communicators of the gospel today. His gift to break down Bible passages in a way that makes them poignantly relevant is unmatched. Listen to his take on this matter of persistent prayer.

> To knock is to stand at God's door. To make yourself available. To climb the steps, cross the porch, stand at the doorway, and volunteer. Knocking goes beyond the realm of thinking and into the realm of acting. To knock is to ask, What can I do? How can I obey? Where can I go?[1]

Persistence is the key. But Jesus goes a step further, instructing us to pray boldly. Listen to this passage from Hebrews.

> Therefore, since we have a great high priest who has gone through the heavens, Jesus the Son of God, let

us hold firmly to the faith we profess. For we do not have a high priest who is unable to sympathize with our weaknesses, but we have one who has been tempted in every way, just as we are—yet was without sin. Let us then approach the throne of grace with confidence, so that we may receive mercy and find grace to help us in our time of need.

—Hebrews 4:14-16

Perhaps a little backstory is in order here for purposes of clarification. In Old Testament times, the high priest was the only person who could enter the Holy of Holies, which represented the place where God kept residence among His people. Behind a thick curtain, this most sacred place housed the Ark of the Covenant and other holy items. Once a year, the high priest would pull back this curtain and enter into the Holy of Holies, symbolically coming into the very presence of God to make atonement for the people. In this passage in Hebrews, Paul is referencing Jesus who is *our* High Priest. By His death and resurrection, Jesus provided for our atonement, in effect pulling back the sacred curtain to give each of us access into the very presence of God.

Coming back to our original question, if you sense that God has not answered a specific prayer yet, then stay on Him! Keep praying, keeping asking, and be bold with your prayers. But as you pray, don't be like the bratty child who plugs his fingers in his ears because he doesn't want to hear what his mommy and daddy are telling him. Sometimes God's answer is no, whether we like it or not. Sometimes the answer is not yet, whether we like it or not. But as we mature in our faith, we learn to trust Him completely, even when we don't like the answers He's given us.

Which leads us to a very important question: How do we go on when God is silent?

Ever feel like your prayers are just bouncing off the ceiling? Frustrating, isn't it? Remember those little super balls you could buy from vending machines? As a child, I used to love those things. You could bounce them to the moon and back. Well, almost. Sometimes it feels like we're tossing our prayers up, and they're bouncing off the ceiling like those super balls. They just keep coming back to us, no matter how many times we toss them up.

Unfortunately, there's nothing even remotely funny about those times when God seems to be missing in action and silent. We've all been there. Times when we must hold on with every ounce of our strength and cling to His promises that He'll never let go of us. If we truly believe He is who He says He is, then we must acknowledge His sovereignty and know within our heart of hearts that what He allows to happen to us always has a purpose. Even on the darkest night. Even when our souls cry out in unspeakable pain. Even when we can't face another day. We hold on because we know He's holding on to us as well.

Babbie Mason wrote a beautiful song called "Trust His Heart." Let me share a few of her lyrics with you.

All things work for our good
Though sometimes we can't see how they could
Struggles that break our hearts in two
Sometimes blind us to the truth
Our Father knows what's best for us
His ways are not our own
So when your pathway grows dim,
And you just don't see Him,

> Remember you're never alone.
> God is too wise to be mistaken,
> God is too good to be unkind.
> So when you don't understand,
> When you don't see his plan,
> When you can't trace his hand,
> Trust his heart.[2]

I've prayed those lyrics time and time again when God seemed silent in my life. I've also prayed them on behalf of others going through difficult times, especially those times when nothing makes any sense at all.

Nashville is known as Music City USA, home to both country music and contemporary Christian music. We're proud of our musical heritage, and we like to think of our hometown celebrities as our own. So it was with a tremendous sense of sadness here in the Nashville area on a spring day in May of 2008 when we heard of the tragic death of little Maria Sue Chapman, the precious adopted daughter of Steven Curtis Chapman and his wife Mary Beth. The circumstances of her death only compounded the grief that washed across our city and the rest of the world. While backing out of their driveway, Maria's eighteen-year-old brother, Will, never saw his little sister in the path of his vehicle. It seemed unthinkable. Unbearable. Such a horrible, freak accident. Why would God allow such a thing to happen? In the weeks and months that followed, the Chapman family's testimony bore witness to their rock-solid belief that the anchor of their faith in God would hold.

But it didn't stop their hearts from aching. After I heard about the Chapman's tragedy, a song by Steven Curtis Chapman kept playing over and over in my head.

Sometimes He comes in the clouds
Sometimes His face can not be found
Sometimes the sky is dark and gray
But some things can only be known
And sometimes our faith can only grow
When we can't see . . .
So sometimes He comes in the clouds
Sometimes He comes in the rain
And we question the pain
And wonder why God can seem so far away . . .[3]

Steven Curtis Chapman wrote that song back in 1995 for an album project that invited several Christian recording artists to put specific lessons from Oswald Chambers' *My Utmost for His Highest* to music. Chapman is a huge Oswald Chambers fan. Such an invitation was surely a labor of love for him. But never in a million years could he have imagined those lyrics he penned would one day be so excruciatingly personal.

We live in an imperfect world filled with imperfect people. Bad things happen to good people. Always have, always will. In 1996, a family friend of ours was bludgeoned to death by her husband of thirty-five years in their Austin, Texas, home. It happened more than a decade ago, long before names like Chandra Levy, Lacy Peterson, or Staci Peterson became familiar to us.

Then there are those other names we recognize—Adam Walsh, Polly Klass, Amber Hagerman (for whom the "Amber Alerts" were named), Elizabeth Smart, Madeline McCann . . . senseless abductions of innocent children, most of them found murdered or never found at all. Or Natalee Holloway, who vanished while on a graduation trip in Aruba. Why would a loving God allow these kinds of things to happen?

Then there are the natural tragedies like the 2004 Indonesian Tsunami. Hurricane Katrina and her many siblings. Tornadoes that bulldoze entire towns off the map. Wildfires and earthquakes. The unbelievable devastation of the flood that occurred here in my hometown of Nashville, Tennessee, just this week!

And then those tragedies of the terrorist variety, like September 11, 2001.

On and on and on it goes. Tragedy will always be a part of life on earth. We may not understand why God allows such things to happen. But we have a choice. Either we can turn our backs on God, even blame Him for these unspeakable heartaches, or we can hold on. We can refuse to let go, even against all odds. Even when our faith is tested beyond our human abilities. Even when nothing makes sense any more. We can hold on because God is our only hope.

Remember when we talked about God's perspective as if He's way up high above our parade in His holy blimp? He's got the better view of your life and mine. He sees it all—every bump and obstacle and detour along our life's path. That's why we can trust Him. That's why we can believe his promise in Isaiah 41:10.

> So do not fear, for I am with you;
> > do not be dismayed, for I am your God.
> I will strengthen you and help you;
> > I will uphold you with my righteous right hand.

God tells us over and over, just hold on! I will provide a way for you! In the darkest night. At the end of all logic and reason. On the brink of utter despair . . . hold on!

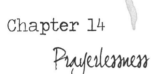

Chapter 14

Prayerlessness

The one concern of the devil is to keep Christians from praying. He fears nothing from prayerless studies, prayerless work, and prayerless religion. He laughs at our toil, mocks at our wisdom, but trembles when we pray.
—Samuel Chadwick

I would be remiss if I spent this entire book talking up the blessings and benefits of prayer without also addressing the polar opposite—prayerlessness. In today's culture, as Christians find themselves constantly ridiculed for their beliefs and practices, it's not hard to connect the dots and understand why so few people actually pray. What's especially sad is that Christians rarely communicate with others about how prayer impacts their daily lives. As if we think only the miraculous prayers are worthy of mention. If someone isn't cured from cancer or a missing child isn't returned safely home, we assume our prayers aren't "big" enough to share with others.

Or perhaps you understand the nuts and bolts of prayer, but admit that this whole prayer thing just isn't your style. The idea of spending time alone with God is just too weird for you, so you've decided you'll take your chances and go it alone.

I'm truly sorry to hear that. I've clearly blown my opportunity on these pages to help you understand this amazing gift called prayer. I'm sorry because you're missing out on one of the greatest blessings you'll ever know.

But just so you know, you're a walking lightning rod for trouble. Consider yourself warned.

A friend once told me about teaching a class at a Christian conference and retreat center. One day after class, one of her class members approached her. He introduced himself and said he was the pastor of a small church in another state. He explained that before he left home he told his congregation that upon his return, he was going to throw out everything they were doing as a church and start practicing some new methods of doing church. My friend was shocked to hear such a declaration. She asked him the first thing that came to her mind. "How are you praying about such drastic measures?" He quickly informed her—in these exact words—"Oh, I'm not much into prayer."

What?! I was flabbergasted when she told me that. How could a pastor, called by God to shepherd a group of believers, not pray? Naturally, I came up with all kinds of witty, sarcastic responses if he'd said such a thing to me. "Kinda full of yourself, aren't you, Pastor No-Pray? Who made *you* God?" I still get rattled just thinking about the audacity of such a statement. A pastor who doesn't pray? Please. Is it any wonder so many churches wither on the vine and have to close their doors because no one comes? Is it any wonder we're so clueless about prayer if our church leaders don't lead by example? Granted, he is just one pastor from one small church. But we all know of churches that are forever split and damaged by pastors who have strayed far from their calling. It's a dangerous position to be in.

Prayerlessness. It's a mouthful, but I have to admit the mere thought of it scares the bejeebies out of me. I wonder what a life totally void of prayer is like. It's one thing to be an atheist who doesn't believe in God, let alone prayer. It's something else entirely to be a believer who doesn't pray.

One of the best examples of prayerlessness I've come across is described in the book I mentioned earlier called *Just Give Me Jesus* by Anne Graham Lotz.[1] She sets the scene for us. Jesus has just completed what would later be known as the Lord's Supper with His disciples. He knows what is about to happen. He knows Judas will betray Him, leading the Roman soldiers to arrest Him. He knows He will be beaten and mocked and nailed to a cross where His physical body will die. Knowing all this, how does Jesus spend His last remaining hours on earth?

He prays.

He takes His disciples with Him to the garden, a place where He often prays. Once there, He tells his disciples to pray "that you may not enter into temptation." I bet the disciples were perplexed at that instruction, don't you? Then again, they were probably used to similar requests from Him. So Jesus leaves them there and goes just a little further where He kneels to pray one of the most heart-wrenching prayers ever recorded.

> "Father, if you are willing, remove this cup from me.
> Nevertheless, not my will, but yours, be done." . . .
> And being in an agony he prayed more earnestly;
> and his sweat was like great drops of blood falling
> down to the ground.
> —Luke 22:42, 44, ESV

Again, Christ knew what was about to transpire, so He readied himself by pouring out His heart before God.

The disciples? Sound asleep. Snoozing away just a few feet from the Lord. Finding them conked out, Jesus scolds them and tells them once again to pray. Can't you see Him shaking His head, wondering why they can't just do what He asked them to? A little while later, He returns and finds them snoring up a storm. Again.

But this time it's too late. At that moment Judas arrives with soldiers and a crowd of priests and other accusers. Judas betrays Jesus with a kiss, selling the Son of God for thirty pieces of silver. But Jesus was prayed up. He didn't fight them or try to make a run for it; He simply allowed it to happen because He knew it was all part of God's will.

The disciples were a whole different story. Lotz puts it this way.

> As the disciples, still rubbing sleep from their eyes, had grasped what was happening, they had abruptly reacted by scurrying in every direction.[2]

Well that's just great, guys. You sleep on the job, then at the first sign of trouble, you run away like a bunch of wimps. All except for one, that is.

> Peter, who had been sleeping when he should have been praying and therefore did not have a clue what the will of God was in this situation, charged the soldiers with his drawn sword. He swiped viciously at the nearest head but only managed to shave off the right ear of Malchus, servant to the high priest. What in the world was Peter doing? . . . Whatever he might have been

thinking, the real reason for his rash behavior was prayerlessness.[3]

What a bonehead! What a sorry excuse for a disciple. And what a stupid thing to do when surrounded by a bunch of armed soldiers. Way to go, Peter. We'll just call you King of the Knee Jerk. Guess you showed them, didn't you?

With all the commotion, Jesus could have easily slipped away from the crowd and made the greatest escape in all of history. But that thought probably never crossed His mind. He immediately scolded Peter—again—shouting, "No more of this!" (Luke 22:51*a*). Then Jesus touched the ear of Malchus, and his ear was healed. I wonder what the angry, accusing crowd thought when they witnessed that miracle? Evidently they weren't too impressed because they still demanded that Jesus be arrested. And, well, you know the rest of the story.

Back up a minute. Tell me something. Be honest. It felt good pointing fingers at those lazy disciples, didn't it? They were the Chosen, hanging out with the Son of God, for crying out loud. And they couldn't keep their eyes open, even for a little while, after the aforementioned Son of God told them to pray? What a bunch of losers! As for Peter? C'mon, admit it. You joined right in when I blasted him for that ridiculous stunt in the garden, cutting off that guy's ear. Anyone with a lick of sense would know that wouldn't help a thing, right?

But hold on. If we're completely honest, don't you and I pull some of those same stunts? Aren't we just as guilty as those sleeping disciples? If we're believers in Christ, we've been commanded to pray. Yet just how faithful are we about praying? We've already discussed the multitude of lame excuses we all use. Hey, I'm as guilty as anyone. I still fight this call to prayer as much as the next guy. I've 'fessed up about my struggle to stay focused in those few minutes I allot God each day. And yes—I, Diane Hale Moody, do hereby admit that I have been known to fall asleep while praying. It happens. I stand guilty before you.

There. I said it. Now it's your turn. Pull back that accusatory finger and take a good long look at yourself. Have you fallen asleep on the job like these disciples? Like me? Have you ignored the urgent call to pray, like these disciples, thereby sabotaging the spiritual preparation for whatever might lie ahead of you?

I've mentioned that my husband runs an Internet filtering company called Hedgebuilders. This service makes it possible to block pornographic sites on the Internet. Originally designed as a Christian filtering service, Hedgebuilders offers this service at cost for those in the ministry. In addition to its regular customers, these ministerial customers include churches, Christian schools, missionaries, pastors, ministers, and many more from all around the world. Rarely a day goes by that Ken doesn't spend time counseling individuals—or their spouses—who are addicted to pornography. The anonymity of the Internet kicked down the last door for those people who would never think to go near an adult bookstore or browse the pages of *Playboy*. Now, with a few clicks, some of the most provocative pictures and videos are available to anyone who wants to find them, all in complete privacy.

Therein lies the problem. The Bible tells us the enemy prowls the earth "like a roaring lion looking for someone to devour" (1 Peter 5:8). What better target than those called as God's messengers—pastors, Bible teachers, Christian school teachers, and the thousands of missionaries around the globe?

You can almost hear the enemy whispering in their ears. *Go on. No one's looking. You work hard. You deserve a little fun now and then. You're not hurting anyone! What could possibly be wrong with gazing at the beauty of God's creation? After all, God designed sexual desire, right? He formed those bodies, didn't He? Go ahead. Your secret's safe with me . . .*

And so it begins. An addiction so powerful some of the most admired preachers of our time have admitted to its stronghold and the damage it has caused them in their ministry, their marriages, and their personal walk with the Lord.

But long, long ago Jesus showed us precisely how to handle the temptations we face in our lives.

He prayed.

After His baptism, Jesus spent forty days and forty nights in the desert fasting and praying. Satan watched and waited, giving those hunger pangs plenty of time to weaken Jesus. Then he approached the Son of God, tempting Him three different times. Each time, Jesus readily rebuked him, quoting scripture to put him in his place, until the enemy finally departed. Jesus withstood the enticements and lures of the evil one because He had prayed (Matthew 4).

Easy for Him, you say. After all, He is the Son of God. You're exactly right. He is God's Son. But He was both fully God and fully human. Meaning, He experienced physical hunger and loneliness and fatigue and heartache and every other human frailty. He experienced all those things and more. And in doing so, He exemplified how we too must handle the temptations we encounter in our lives.

No temptation has overtaken you that is not common to man. God is faithful, and he will not let you be tempted beyond your ability, but with the

temptation he will also provide the way of escape,
that you may be able to endure it.

—1 Corinthians 10:13, ESV

He's been there. He knows. And He's provided for our every need. If only we'll be obedient. If only we'll stay on our knees before God, arming ourselves with His protection and His power and strength to withstand any temptation. If only we'll heed His call to pray.

If only.

Chapter 15
The Power of Prayer

> *For God has not given us a spirit of fear,*
> *but of power and of love and of a sound mind.*
> —2 TIMOTHY 1:7, NKJV

f only we'll heed His call to prayer. Sounds like a challenge, doesn't it? As if someone has drawn a line in the sand and dared us to stick a big hairy toe over it. (For the record, my toes aren't hairy, so it must be yours.) But have you ever wondered what this old world would be like if we actually heeded God's call to prayer? Have you ever fully grasped the power of prayer we have at our disposal?

Ever hear of Dwight L. Moody? I'd love to tell you D. L. Moody is on some branch of my husband's family tree, but alas, he is not. My father-in-law, Art Moody, sold shoes, as did Dwight when he was a young man, but that's about as far as it goes. Regardless, I like to think of him as Uncle Dwight. Let me tell you about him.

Dwight Moody was a colorful nineteenth-century evangelist who rose from utter poverty to become one of the greatest preachers of the gospel of all times. He was founder of the Moody Bible Institute, Moody Church, and Moody Publishers in Chicago. I've always thought the story of Moody's life would make a fascinating movie. By all measures, he was a just simple, ordinary man. But when this Massachusetts native was thirty-four years old, he visited Dublin, Ireland, where fellow evangelist Henry Varley said something he would never forget. "Moody, the world has yet to see what God will do with a man fully consecrated to Him." It is told that Moody mulled over the statement, repeating it to himself several times. Realizing that there was no requirement for such a man to be educated or scholarly, Moody finally responded, "Well, by the Holy Spirit in me, I'll be that man!"[1]

He became the embodiment of an ordinary life used by God to do extraordinary things. Over 100 million people across two different continents would hear him preach. Thousands of lives would be forever changed by the message of salvation he preached. He reached downtrodden street kids and sailors in port, as well as the millionaires, royalty, and political leaders of his time. The message was the same to all: God loves you.

But those who knew him well often said he was a far greater pray-er than preacher. After Moody's death in 1923, his closest friend, Dr. R. A. Torrey, was asked to speak at a memorial service for him. In that famous sermon, Torrey said, "He was a man who met every difficulty that stood in his way—by prayer. Everything he undertook was backed up by prayer, and in everything, his ultimate dependence was upon God."[2]

Granted, you and I may never be the spiritual giant of faith that Moody was. But that same power is available to us today. Have you ever known someone whose heart was sold out to God, whose life was firmly rooted on their knees in prayer? Someone whose prayers made a significant difference in the lives of those around them?

With your permission, I'd like to tell you a very personal story. I lost my mother to colon cancer in April of 2007. She was eighty-two at the time of her death. We've always been a very close-knit family, so when she was first diagnosed with Stage IV colon cancer, we were devastated. The cancer had already spread to her liver and stomach. My sister and I were shocked to learn that Mom and Dad's beloved doctor had never once suggested they have a colonoscopy. How could there be such negligence when early detection through colonoscopy can often prevent cancer? But anger and heartache would never stop the disease that had already ravaged her body. Still, she was convinced she could beat it. At first, she was able to tolerate the chemotherapy. But the cumulative effects of the treatment soon took their toll. Hospice graciously stepped in to provide in-home care.

In what can only be called a divine appointment, my sister and I had made plans to visit Mom and Dad at home in Tulsa the week following Easter of that year. We'd made our flight reservations back in January thinking we'd go help our parents start packing for their upcoming move to Nashville where they'd be near us. The day we arrived at the house, the hospice aide had just given Mom a bath, and she was just coming out of her bedroom. It was a little startling to see her using a walker, but we were so pleased to see her up and about. She was on some pretty heavy pain medication, so we talked only briefly before she dozed off on the couch.

Little did we know that would be our last conversation with her. She slept around the clock for the next few days, not eating or drinking. By Friday night, she lapsed into a coma, her chest giving up what is called the death rattle—a sound I hope I never hear again. It was necessary to suction out her nose and mouth every twenty minutes or so, so we took turns staying by her side around the clock. We sang some of her favorite hymns and talked to her as if she could hear every word. One night when I was curled up in bed beside her, I began to tell her how much she meant to me and how much I loved her. We'd had so many wonderful memories together.

Then I remembered a time in my life that wasn't so wonderful. A memory I hadn't thought about in decades, but one that forever changed the course of my life. It was the year I'd graduated from college. After an emotionally rough summer, I moved to Memphis, Tennessee, where my sister lived. I'd been corresponding with my ex-boyfriend's best friend (never, never a good idea—trust me on that). "Danny" was in the Navy stationed in Hawaii at the time.

Over the course of time we fell in love and got engaged. I should back up and tell you that at this point in my life, I'd strayed far, far away from the Lord. Which, of course, explains why I was so easily able to turn a blind eye to the numerous warning flags surrounding me. I was head over heels in love with the most romantic man I'd ever known. The wedding plans rushed full steam ahead—invitations printed, the date reserved at the church, wedding gown alterations complete, bridesmaids and groomsmen lined up. Danny would be deployed for six months not long after we married, but I felt confident I would enjoy being a Navy wife.

Then one Saturday morning, just a couple months before our wedding, I woke up and found a letter from Mom in my mailbox. I was surprised at how thick the letter was since we talked several times a week by phone. As I began to read Mom's letter, something happened to me. It's hard to put into words, but it was almost as if a window had just been opened, allowing a breeze of fresh air to wash over me. The blinders came off as the truth of my mother's words penetrated my heart.

You see, my fiancé was not a believer. He was also an alcoholic, though I'd refused to admit it. And when I mentioned that he was the most romantic man I'd ever known, he came by it quite naturally, with a past that included a girl in every port, and then some. But I had convinced myself none of that mattered. He loved me and wanted to marry me, and that was enough.

It wasn't Danny's fault. It was completely mine. Danny was who he'd always been—my hilarious, fun-loving, handsome sailor who traveled the world. But I was not the person I'd always been. I'd turned my back on God, becoming someone far removed from the shy girl who'd grown up in church and given her life to Christ. What a mess I'd made of my life.

Mom wasn't telling me not to marry him. She was reminding me who I was and the commitment I'd made giving my life to Christ so many years ago. She asked me hard questions about the life I would soon be leading as a Navy wife. She could have ranted at me and quoted a thousand scripture verses, but she didn't. It wasn't her way. Instead, she simply loved me enough to take an enormous risk. My father recently told me how hard it was for her to send me that letter. He said she wrestled with it for a long time, worrying that I might respond with anger at her intrusion, permanently damaging our relationship.

Dad also told me how fervently she prayed over that letter before she mailed it.

With tears streaming down my face as I read and reread the letter, I finally reached for the phone and called Mom. I sobbed and sobbed before I could finally thank her for helping me see the mistake I was about to make. I thanked her for loving me enough to take the risk she'd taken. In fact, that very day Dad put her on a plane to Memphis to spend some time with me. She prayed with me before I made the call to my sailor, calling off our wedding. She held me as I cried both tears of heartache and tears of relief.

The tender memories of that chapter in my life washed over me that late night as I talked to Mom, her physical life drawing ever closer to an end. I needed to make sure she knew how grateful I was that God had used her to draw me back to Him. I needed to tell her how thankful I was that God had blessed me with a mother who understood tough love. I needed to let her know how much I appreciated the depth of love she'd always given me through all of my life, even when I was quite unlovable. Two days later, on April 16, 2007, we said our good-byes as my mother passed from this life into the presence of her Lord and Savior.

So you see, I'm more than just a little passionate about the power of prayer. I'm living proof of it. My marriage is living proof of it. My children are living proof of it. The Bible tells us, "The effective, fervent prayer of a righteous man avails much" (James 5:16*b*, NKJV). *The Message* puts it this way: "The prayer of a person living right with God is something powerful to be reckoned with." I can certainly vouch for that in my life. Can you?

Prayer changes things. But I think it's actually much more than that. Listen to this quote from Oswald Chambers.

> To say that "prayer changes things" is not as close to the truth as saying, "Prayer changes me and then I change things." God has established things so that prayer, on the basis of redemption, changes the way a person looks at things.[3]

In other words, it's not so much a matter of "things" being changed as it is a change in the way we perceive those things, then act upon them. Do you think you and I will ever fully embrace or understand that kind of prayer power? Will we ever take God at His word and tap into this kind of life-changing power?

If I were to draw that line in the sand and ask you to heed the call to prayer, would you? And if you did, what kind of changes would be possible in your life? In the lives of those around you? Is there anything holding you back from making a commitment to become serious about your prayer life? If there is, get on your knees. Right here, right now. Offer it up to God, asking Him to forgive you for letting it stand between you and Him. Then bare your soul before Him and ask Him to help you learn how to be a more serious and committed pray-er. Then get ready to see how He will transform your heart and change your life forever!

Chapter 16
Final Confessions from My Stacker's Heart

For I do not understand my own actions.
For I do not do what I want,
but I do the very thing I hate.
—Romans 7:15, ESV

Go ahead. Admit it. You thought this was going to be a boring book on a subject you were only partially interested in. You thought you'd read a few pages and that would be that. But if you've made it this far, I'm guessing that maybe—just maybe—something on these pages struck a chord with you. Maybe you started seeing Jesus sitting in *your* den, coffee in hand, waiting patiently to spend time with you. Maybe you found out prayer wasn't so much about style as it was opening your heart and communicating with God. Maybe for the first time, you discovered a genuine hunger for something more in your relationship with God. Like making more time for Him in your oh-so-busy life. Or better yet, maybe you finally made the decision to move out of the pilot's seat and let Him take over the controls of your life. Maybe you've begun to wonder what your life would look like if that really happened.

Remember when you were back in school and as class began your teacher would say those two dreaded words:

pop quiz? Well, boys and girls, put away your notes, get out a clean sheet of paper, and let's see how you're doing. Second thought, don't think of it as a test so much as a spiritual barometer to see what kind of progress you've made. Caution: Be brave. I'm aiming right for the jugular with this one.

If someone told you to spend the next twenty-four hours in prayer, what's your first response? Be honest now.

1. I can't. My schedule is booked solid from now until forever. No way.

2. *Noooooooo! Puhleeeeeez* don't make me! I'd lose my mind having to sit still for that long! Besides, I'm hypoglycemic. No can do.

3. I think I'm having a heart attack. I need to get to the hospital. (Actually, what you're feeling is nothing more than an intense inner-shuddering; but a heart attack sounds more serious, right?)

4. Wow! That sounds amazing! I've always wanted to do something like that! Let me grab my Bible, and I'm good to go!

Think about answer number 4. I imagine it something akin to a military wife whose soldier husband is headed home after eighteen months in the Middle East. The prospect of spending time with him for twenty-four uninterrupted hours thrills her heart. She's excited and eager and filled with anticipation!

Okay, now put that back into the context of spending twenty-four hours alone with your Father, your Lord, your Savior. Are you excited and eager? Are you filled with anticipation of all that's in store for you? Would you be surprised to learn that some people actually *do* that? Do you know some people have even spent forty days and forty nights in prayer and fasting? And not just preachers or pastors, regular people like you and me. So I ask you once again. Is there even a trace of desire or yearning to block off twenty-four hours to spend with God? Good question. And whatever answer is milling about in your heart and head should give you some indication of where you are spiritually. That's a lot to think about, isn't it?

Another confession. One for the road, if you will. I love Sunday afternoons. It's the one time all week I can veg without guilt and nap while blissfully claiming my official "day of rest." That's biblical, right? And once we get home from church and have lunch, I love to curl up on the sofa and watch hours of football, golf, baseball, or some old movies in the off-seasons. I look at that block of time—whether it's three or four hours for a Titans' game or five to six hours of the final round of PGA golf—as my very own kick-back-and-relax time. After a long week, I deserve it, right? And if I drift off for a snooze, even better! Have I mentioned I love my Sunday afternoons?

Now. Let me make that pop quiz more personal. If I sensed God nudging me to give up my leisurely Sunday after-noons and spend them in prayer with Him, would I? If He asked me to give those long glorious hours of R&R over to Him for prayer, would I willingly submit to His request? Is there any way I'd actually be happy to do that?

No. I'm cringing here because I hate to admit it to you after all we've been through on these pages, but no. In my heart of hearts, I know I'd do it but with a serious grudge. If I did it at all.

Oh, I might not hesitate to block off a twenty-four-hour chunk of time to pray—if the price tag said "one time only." But once a year? Once a month? I dunno. Maybe . . .

They say confession is good for the soul, but the reality is, it sickens me to admit this is where I am. After all I've learned and all He's taught me . . . apparently I'm still greedy about my precious time. Apparently my spiritual barometer still needs a lot of work.

Still, if you and I are at least willing to start examining our hearts about these matters, we're surely making progress. The challenge is to move beyond retrospection and do something about it. Amen?

There's so much more to learn about prayer. We've barely scratched the surface here, folks. That was intentional on my part because I made a conscious effort to focus on two specific things: (1) learning what prayer is and isn't, and (2) learning how to establish a routine, daily prayer time.

Bottom line, I can tell you this (now that you bought my book and read it)—none of it matters. Not the methods, not the verses, not the list of reasons for praying, not the clever and quirky chats we've had—none of it. That's because the only thing that matters is this: *that you pray.* Every. Single. Day. Focused and fully concentrating on your relationship with God through prayerful communication.

I have to be honest. A funny thing happens whenever you try to tackle a subject like this, to inform or inspire "others." In the end you quickly discover the vastness of your subject, and you're immediately humbled by how much you don't know about it. That's certainly been the case for me as I've shared some of my own experiences with you. But I'll make a few final confessions, like this one—and I'm utterly embarrassed to tell you. While burning up my keyboard, pontificating about my own prayer journey, I've found myself struggling to follow my own advice. Days slipped by before I realized I'd actually skipped my morning prayer times. I'd raced right past my Jesus as He sat in that study, his coffee grown cold.

Am I a hypocrite or what?

And once again, I'm saddened to discover I'm still not the prayer warrior I want to be. Not even close.

Then there are the days I've kept my morning coffee time with Jesus; but if I'm honest, I've done nothing more than go through the motions. I've read some scripture, raced through my prayer journal, and patted myself on the back for being so disciplined. But nothing penetrated my mind, much less my heart. It's that pesky auto-pilot habit we talked about.

But today's stupid blooper takes the cake, the cupcake, the coffee cake, and every other kind of cake in the bakery. At least for me. Oh, I kept my divine appointment this time. But just as I finished reading a scripture passage and started working my way through my prayer journal, I happened to glance over at my cell phone on the end table beside me . . . *I'm really tired of my ringtone. I still love that movie theme song, but it's getting old. I should download a new one. Hmm. What would be a good song? Something by Sting? A Big Band tune? Wait, maybe an old Billy Joel tune . . .*

At that point, I dropped my head in resignation. *Oh no. Not again.*

Don't roll your eyes. I know it may sound silly to you to stress over something so trivial. But at this point in my prayer journey, I should be way, way past this kind of thing by now. Will I never learn? Here I am—an aspiring author working on a book about prayer—so easily and outright distracted, so easily lured away from my oh-so meaningful prayer life by nothing more than a simple glance at my cell phone. Good grief! I'm no different than that bored little freckle-faced mini-me at Camp Nunny Cha-Ha so many years ago—unable to keep focus and pray. Unable to do any of those things I've been writing about for months. Will I ever conquer these distractions? Why can't I just do as I say? Why can't I stay focused for even a lousy twenty minutes? Have I made no headway at all after all these years?

Oh no. Here it comes again. Prayer guilt.

If someone gave out awards for this particular accomplishment, I'd surely be basking in the glory of red-carpet praise. I'd make my way to the stage when my name was announced as the All-Time Queen of Prayer Guilt. Got the tiara, got the trophy, got the guilt.

Call me a drama queen, but you get the point. Then, while I'm busily slapping a Prayer Slacker sticker on my worn and tattered guilt-trip suitcase, I start thinking about David. You know, the one from the Old Testament. The shepherd who became a king. But David was hardly a saint. Among his many virtues, he was also a peeping Tom, an adulterer, a murderer, a schemer, and a sorry excuse for a father. Yet God referred to David as "a man after [my] own heart" (1 Samuel 13:14). Doesn't make sense, does it? I mean, those were big sins David committed!

Isn't it odd how we label those "big sins" to cover things like murder, adultery, child abuse, kidnapping, terrorism, arson, Ponzy scheming, and the like? It's as if we play a game called "My Sin vs. Your Sin." My little white lie to my friend is way better than you stealing a fiver out of someone's purse. My "creative" bookkeeping is nowhere near as bad as you cheating on your husband. And on and on it goes. We start to feel rather smug about our little sins in light of someone else's mega-sins. It's actually kind of sick to think of it in those terms—having pride about the fact that I'm not as bad a sinner as you. Oh, the twists and turns of human logic.

But it completely messes with our minds to think that God views all sins equally. A sin is a sin is a sin in His eyes. And the fact remains, we all sin. But we're children of a loving Father who yearns to forgive us if only we'll come clean and confess those sins, big or small. In other words, He loves me even when I forget to pray. He loves me even when I just go through the motions. And He loves me even when I screw up royally like David did.

Having kids is a sure-fire way to learn about the full depth of forgiveness. We may hate some of the choices they make. We may grieve over the idiotic, repetitive mistakes they make and the resulting consequences they must face. But we still love them. No matter what, we still love them. Now take that unconditional love you feel for your kids and multiply it by a couple trillion. That still doesn't come close to the love God has for us. Even when we screw up.

So, hey, maybe one of the reasons I've continued to blow it in my own prayer life is so that you can learn from my pathetic mistakes. Yeah. I'm sure that's it. But wait—there's more! (Channeling the late Billy Mays here.) There's another potential danger lurking around us if we actually follow through and keep our daily appointment with God. It creeps up when we least expect it. We're cruising along, day after day, faithfully making time for God in our routine, feeling all warm and fuzzy about ourselves . . . then BAM! That's when it happens.

> Your god may be your little Christian habit—the
> habit of prayer or Bible reading at certain times of
> your day. Watch how your Father will upset your
> schedule if you begin to worship your habit instead
> of what the habit symbolizes. We say, "I can't do that
> right now; this is my time alone with God." No, this
> is your time alone with your habit.[1]

Ouch?! That's another one from Oswald Chambers. Ol' Ozzie doesn't mince words, does he? I don't know about you, but that one felt like I just had my knuckles whacked by a nun with a ruler. Which is particularly strange since I never went to Catholic school.

But Oswald is right. It's so very easy to fall into this trap of worshiping our habit of praying. It's that stupid pride monster rearing its ugly head yet again. My pastor once said "I stink at prayer because I'm so good at pride."[2] Pete, I think most of us are in same boat with you on that one. In fact, that boat's starting to sink because so many of us are crowded on it with you!

Professor and author Dr. Calvin Miller writes this word of caution: "Remember anything more important than God to you, *is* god to you.[3]

Whoa. Think about that one for a moment. It holds all kinds of implications, doesn't it? See, the minute you and I begin to think we've learned all there is to know about this or that, and fancy ourselves as some self-proclaimed authority on the subject, we're doomed. Especially in matters of faith. There is only one Authority, and His name is Jehovah. Our God. Our Lord Jesus Christ. Our Heavenly Father. The rest of us will never fully get it until we meet Him face to face. And, oh, what a moment that will be!

In the meantime, we do our best to live our lives to honor Him. And there's no better way to do that than spending time with Him. Every single day. Not as some kind of robotrons, programmed to meet a set schedule. But as children of God, who hunger to spend time with Him, opening our hearts to Him.

By now you know I'm not perfect. But neither are you, my friend. In fact, I'll bet the reason this book interested you was because the title touched a nerve. Am I right? If so, you're probably a confessed (or as yet un-confessed) slacker just like me. We've both failed time and time again. And guess what? We'll continue to fail time and time again. So what can we do about that? You need to learn as I have learned that each day is a new day, a new beginning with a clean slate. Repeat that out loud with me.

Each day is a new day,
a new beginning with a clean slate.

If your memory struggles like mine, you might want to write that across the inside of your prayer journal or print it and tape it to the edge of your computer screen. Anyplace where you'll see it daily. We need to remind ourselves of that fact every morning as we wake. If we fall into slackerdom for a day or two or three, we just need to try harder today. Then tomorrow. And every tomorrow to follow.

If you'll allow me one final personal note, I want to bring my journey full circle for you. To do so, I need to share a verse with you that always gives me a thrill when I read it. Let me set the scene for you. Early in Jesus' ministry, He began calling His first disciples. One day, He was standing by a lake when a large crowd started pressing in all around Him. They'd heard of His miracles and were anxious to hear more. He saw two boats anchored nearby, but the fishermen were away from them, washing out their nets onshore. So Jesus climbed into one of the boats and told the fisherman named Simon (we know him later as Peter), to put out a little from the shore. Simon obliged, then Jesus sat down and began to teach the people from the boat.

When He finished, He told Simon, "Put out into deep water, and let down the nets for a catch" (Luke 5:4). Simon answers, "Master, we've worked hard all night and haven't caught anything." Now, knowing what we know from later accounts about Simon/Peter (aka Mr. Knee Jerk), can't you just imagine the body language that accompanied his response? Remember, at this point he has no idea who this man is who's telling him what to do. He's exhausted and frustrated after fishing all night and not catching a thing. No doubt he rolls his eyes and throws his shoulders back, posturing at the audacity of such a suggestion, maybe snapping his neck to one side then the other with irritation. *Who does this guy think he is, telling me how to fish?!*

Still, in the last half of that verse, we're told Simon added, "But because you say so, I will let down the nets." What?! Why would a tough guy like Simon cave so quickly to a complete stranger? We're not told, but somehow I like to think it was something he saw in Jesus' eyes. Someone once said the eyes are windows to the soul. And don't you know Jesus had the most captivating, beautiful eyes ever given to a human? Don't you know the immense depth of His love shone through those amazing eyes to everyone He met? Which could possibly explain why Simon so quickly acquiesced and did as he was told. Look what happened.

> When they had done so, they caught such a large number of fish that their nets began to break. So they signaled their partners in the other boat to come and help them, and they came and filled both boats so full that they began to sink.
>
> —Luke 5:6-7

For me, the nugget of truth that speaks to my heart in this passage is the message that if only I'll go deeper in my trust and faith in Him, the more wonders I'll behold in my life—things so far beyond my imagination, I can barely comprehend!

And that has been exactly what has happened. The book you now hold in your hands is evidence of that. I had struggled for years trying to get published. I kept writing novels and wondering why on earth no one was interested in publishing them. One of them, which I wrote in installments on a website, registered more than 67,000 readers and flooded my inbox with more than 1,000 positive e-mails! Still, nothing. An entire decade flew by as I banged my head against my desk, frustrated that my dream wasn't happening.

That was until God finally got my attention. I shared that story with you in the first chapters of this book. Slowly, as I began making time to spend with Him each morning, I realized how much I'd been missing. He had so much to say to me! Why had I never stopped and listened before? Weeks turned into months, months into years, until the time I spent with Him each morning became a daily habit, one that I looked forward to and rarely missed. And in the process, I began to sense God was nudging me about this whole prayer journey I'd been on. I started making notes during my prayer times, writing down verses that God seemed to be showing me and excerpts from books I was reading along the way. At the same time, I was meeting new Christians who had no idea how to have a prayer life with God.

And that's when I knew: God was calling me to write *for Him!* He wanted me to share my story! He wanted me to use the gifts He'd given me—this undying passion for writing, and maybe even the quirky way I visualize situations in my mind—to help others discover the joy and blessings that await them if only they'd make time for Him too. So I started writing. And the words and ideas and examples and scripture verses literally flooded my mind, almost to the point I could barely keep up on my keyboard.

About this time, I met with an editor to tell her about my novel—the story I told you about with the huge online following. In the midst of our conversation, I mentioned this non-fiction book about prayer that God had literally laid in my lap. Not only did she want to publish it, she also bought my novel!

Oh. My. Gosh.

Friend, you may not give a rat's patootie about writing a book or getting published. But I'm here to tell you I felt like I was the living embodiment of that verse in Luke 5:4. God had told me to go deep when He drew me to Himself, teaching me how to have a prayer life with Him, and now He was over-whelming me with blessings in ways I could *never* have imagined. So I have to ask. What will it take for you to go deep with God? All those silly excuses aside, what's stopping you?

I know you'll be shocked that I'm finally going to wrap this up and leave the rest to you. I thank you for taking time to read about my prayer journey. I'm flattered—dare I say shocked—that you picked my book off the shelf when there are so many other authors far more qualified from which to choose.

No wait. I take that back. There may be hundreds of authors more qualified on the subject of prayer, but concerning prayer slackerdom? No way. I'm it. Self-proclaimed with moun-tains of guilt to show for it. Although, thankfully, I have a Father who graciously forgives me for all my stupid blunders along the way, wiping my slate clean whenever I come to Him in humble apology. He offers you the exact same forgiveness. It's there for the taking.

I hope in some small way, you've been challenged enough to start on a prayer journey of your own. I pray that you'll accept the challenge and find out for yourself what a differ-ence daily personal prayer can make in your life. I guarantee you'll never be the same. You have my word on that.

Call to Me, and I will answer you, and show you great and mighty things, which you do not know.

—Jeremiah 33:3, NKJV

Study Questions

Introduction

1. Have you ever had a Come-to-Jesus moment in your life? If so, what was the unique path that led you to Him? If not, have you ever experienced that tug in your heart and wondered what it was?
2. When was the last time you had a consistent prayer life? How long did it last? Why do you think you succeeded?
3. If it's no longer a part of your life, why is that?

1. My Personal Prayer Journey

1. What is your earliest memory concerning prayer?
2. When did you first learn about having a *personal* prayer life?

2. My Journey Continues

1. Have you ever shaken your fist at God?

2. Nicole Johnson talks about spectator living. Are you living as a spectator? What dreams are you ignoring so you won't face disappointment?

3. Excuses, Excuses, Excuses

1. Which of the Top 10 Excuses hit closest to home for you?
2. Have you ever fully comprehended that God made you because He wants to have a relationship with you? Does that change how you regard His intimate love for you?

4. More Excuses?

1. Did a seemingly unanswered prayer ever affect your love for God?
2. Have you ever shunned God because your M&Ms didn't drop down in the vending machine after you deposited your coins (translation: prayed)?
3. Be honest. Are you lazy when it comes to God?

5. Our Number 1 Excuse for Not Praying

1. Are you too busy for God?
2. What does discipline look like in your relationship with God?
3. So, on average, how many hours a day do you watch TV? Hmm? (Don't forget to include those morning news programs.)

6. Just How Badly Do You Want It?

1. Well, then, just how badly do you want it?

2. Like Briana in the skit, do you routinely exclude God from your life and your activities? How so?

3. Are you sincerely willing for God to do heart surgery on you? If not, what's stopping you?

7. Getting Started

1. Try to visualize Jesus waiting for you to spend time with Him each day. Where is He? In your home? Outdoors? In your office? Does that visualization help remind you to pray?

2. When is the best time of day for you to meet with God?

8. Gotta-Haves

1. When was the last time you read a Bible?

2. Do you have a readable translation?

3. How would you set up your prayer journal to make the most of your prayer time?

9. Getting to Know Your God

1. Did you learn anything new about God by studying some of the names of God?

2. If you had to pick one of the names we discussed, which one has the most significance to you at this point in your life? Why?

3. Can you think of a specific situation in which you saw God's provision, exemplifying His name of Jehoval-Jireh—The Lord Will Provide?

10. God's Love Letter to You

1. What does abiding in Christ look like in your own life?
2. In your spiritual walk with Christ, are you a:
    - babe in spiritual diapers, still sucking on a pacifier?
    - toddler, still crawling around with no direction, still sucking your thumb?
    - adolescent, focused completely on having fun?
    - teenager, consumed with yourself and little else?
    - adult, maturing in your faith and hungering after God?
3. What has prevented you from studying the Bible up until now?
4. What's your favorite book in the Bible? Don't have one? Ready to find one?

11. In Search of Your "Want-To"

1. After reading the excerpt from Psalm 139, what did you learn about God's love for you?
2. How can we recalibrate our thinking to stop expecting God to join our team and instead focus on joining His team when we pray?

12. The Lord's Prayer 101

1. Okay, be honest. Have you ever really prayed the Lord's Prayer? Or do you just repeat memorized words when you say it?

2. If you could see your prayers in print, would they be hastily written chicken-scratch shorthand? Or are they carefully written from the heart?

13. When God Is Silent

1. When God seems silent, how long is your grace period toward Him before your patience runs out?
2. In the face of unspeakable tragedy, would your faith hold on? Will you cling to God's promises, able to "trust His heart" even when you can't "trace His hand?"

14. Prayerlessness

1. Were you appalled to read about that preacher who admitted he's not much into prayer? But are you equally appalled at your own lack of prayer? (Lose the guilt. Answer the question.) If not, why not?
2. Are you like Peter and the other disciples who fell asleep on the job instead of praying? Why is it we have so much trouble making prayer a priority?

15. The Power of Prayer

1. Are you willing to heed the call to prayer with your heart, mind, and soul?
2. What's keeping you from selling out to God?
3. Do you have any secret dreams you've long neglected because you were too afraid to even pray about them?

16. Final Confessions from My Slacker's Heart

1. How'd you do on that pop quiz? So, what if God actually did ask you to spend twenty-four hours with Him? Or eight hours? Or two? Be honest. Would you freak out?

2. I told you how much I cherish my Sunday afternoons. How about you? Is there something you would not willingly give up if He asked you to?

3. Do you fully comprehend the level of forgiveness God offers you whenever you screw up? Are you willing to accept His forgiveness?

Final Question:

1. After reading this book, are you ready to commit to God to spend time with Him each day? More important, will you?

How to
Become a Christian

If there has never been a time when you invited Jesus into your life to be your Lord and Savior, I would be honored to tell you how. It's really very simple, but you need to know it's a very serious commitment. That means you need to open your heart and come clean before God. But don't worry. He already knows every inch of your heart. He just wants you to be willing to give it to Him completely.

It's important to know that God created us for one purpose: to have a loving relationship with Him. Most of us want to be our own boss because we grow up thinking the world revolves around us. But there can be only one boss, and that is God. In Romans 3:23 we're told that we've all sinned. All of us. That means you and me. And as long as there is sin in our lives, we're separated from God.

But God had a plan. He made a way for us to bridge that gap by giving us His Son Jesus Christ. Romans 6:23 says, "The wages of sin is death, but the gift of God is eternal life in Christ Jesus our Lord."

So how do I follow His plan?

1. First, I admit that God has not been Lord of my life, and then confess my sins. He has promised to forgive us: "If we confess our sins, he is faithful and just and will forgive us our sins and purify us from all unrighteousness" (1 John 1:9).
2. I acknowledge that Jesus died to pay for my sins. "But God demonstrates his own love for us in this: While we were still sinners, Christ died for us" (Romans 5:8).
3. I receive God's free gift of salvation. "For it is by grace you have been saved, through faith—and this not from yourselves, it is the gift of God—not by works, so that no one can boast" (Ephesians 2:8-9).
4. Finally, I invite Jesus to be the Lord of my life. "Everyone who calls on the name of the Lord will be saved" (Romans 10:13).

Commitment to Christ is a personal decision you have to make. It's not something decided for you by your parents or family or friends. It's just between you and God. If you believe that you are ready to make this most important decision you'll ever make—to invite Jesus into your heart to be your Lord and Savior—then all you need to do is pray this simple prayer.

Dear Lord Jesus,
Thank you for loving me even when I was unlovable and ignored You. I realize now how much I need You in my life. I know that I am a sinner, and I'm sorry for the things I've done that I shouldn't have. As best I know how, I ask for Your forgiveness. Please come into my heart and cleanse my life. I

believe that You died on the cross and rose from the grave to give me life. I know You are the only way to God. In this moment, I give my life to You and ask You to help me live a life that honors You. Amen.

Congratulations! Did you know that all of heaven is rejoicing in your decision to become a child of God? That means there's a party going on in your honor right now! Let me be the first to welcome you to the family of God, my friend. And this is just the beginning! It's so important to learn more about the Lord you have just committed your life to, and the best way to do that is to find a Bible-believing church where you can study His Word and surround yourself with others in the family of God. Don't be afraid to shop around until you find a congregation that is sold out to Christ. Then get involved and start your journey in a fellowship of believers living for Christ!

Now, do me one more favor. If you made this most-important life decision, would you let me know? You can write me at *dianehalemoody@gmail.com.*

Acknowledgments

I can honestly say this book is the direct result of some holy nudging on the part of God. Over and over, He showed me why I needed to share my story, to the point I finally tossed aside the novel I was writing and began to write what He had put on my heart. For any life that may be touched by these pages, I give Him the glory.

To Fred and Cathy Weisbrodt and Rick and Beth Herrin, thank you for your friendship and asking the tough questions along the way. We love doing community with you!

To my pastor, Pete Wilson, thank you for inspiring not only me and our entire church family at Nashville's Cross Point Community Church, but also thousands more through-out "the uttermost parts of the earth" through your blog and always-colorful tweets. Thank you for always being the real deal. And for the record, it's obviously not in your DNA to be bland or boring. You're the best.

What a blast it's been to work with Joan Shoup and Joy DeKok at Sheaf House Publishers! Never have two editors made the process so much fun. For all the personal SH attention, brainstorming, and encouragement, a million thanks. Ladies, our next breakfast at Cracker Barrel is on me!

A huge hug and thanks to my amazing daughter, Hannah Schmitt, who designed the perfect cover for my first book. If ever a picture said it all, you knocked this one out of the park, sweetie!

To my son, Ben, thanks for believing in me and showing me by example how passion for something can propel you to accomplish your goals in life. I love you, buddy!

To my YaYa's—Debbie Church, Carol McFarland, and Teresa Nardozzi—thank you for being my own personal cheerleaders along the way and reminding me to never, never give up. Love you, Sistahs!

To my real-life sister, Morlee Maynard, thank you for being my lifelong friend and ever-faithful sounding board. Do you know what a hero you are to me?

To Glenn and Anita Hale, my precious parents who raised me on a solid foundation of faith and taught me the true meaning of unconditional love. How I miss you, Mom.

Every writer needs a buddy in the trenches, and I'm thankful beyond words for Sally Wilson. Sally, thanks for your wonderful friendship, honest critiques, hilarious sense of humor, and all our coffee breaks at the Red Tree in Kingston Springs. I thank God for crossing our paths in Houston so many years ago. Who knew a name tag at a writer's conference could spark such a cherished friendship?

And last but not least, I dedicate this book to Ken—my husband, my best friend, and the love of my life. Thank you for not only believing in me and helping me to see this dream come true; but more important, for your quiet and humble example as a godly man who begins and ends each day on his knees in prayer. How I love doing life with you!

Notes

Introduction

    1. Whittaker Chambers, *Witness* (Washington, D.C.: Regnery Publishing, Inc., 1978), 16-17. All rights reserved. Reprinted by special permission of Regnery Publishing, Inc., Washington, D.C.

2. My Journey Continues

    1. Reprinted by permission. *Fresh-Brewed Life: A Stirring Invitation to Wake Up Your Soul,* Nicole Johnson, © 1999, Thomas Nelson, Inc. Nashville, Tenn. All rights reserved. Page 38.

    2. Ibid., 41.

    3. Ibid., 48.

3. Excuses, Excuses, Excuses

    1. Reprinted by permission. *Just Give Me Jesus,* Anne Graham Lotz, © 2000, Thomas Nelson, Inc. Nashville, Tenn. All rights reserved. Page 10.

4. More Excuses?

    1. Taken from *My Utmost for His Highest* by Oswald Chambers, edited by James Reimann, © 1992 by Oswald Chambers Publications Assn., Ltd., and used by permission of Discovery House Publishers, Grand Rapids Mich. 49501. All rights reserved. August 4 entry.

    2. Quote from *Syncing Through Prayer,* sermon by Pastor Pete Wilson, Cross Point Community Church, Nashville, Tenn.; July 2008.

    3. Ibid.

    4. Ibid.

    5. Chambers, *My Utmost,* August 6.

5. Our Number 1 Excuse for Not Praying

1. Reprinted by permission. *Blue Like Jazz*, Donald Miller, © 2003, Thomas Nelson Inc. Nashville, Tenn. All rights reserved. Page 13.

2. Reprinted by permission. *Second Calling: Finding Passion and Purpose for the Rest of Your Life*, Dale Hanson Bourke, © 2006, Thomas Nelson, Inc. Nashville, Tennessee. All rights reserved. Page 53.

3. John Kirk, *The Mother of the Wesleys: A Biography* (London: Henry James Tresidder, 1864), 186.

4. Chrysalis Blog. *Spotlight on Mom: Susannah Wesley*, February 1, 2007 http://chrysaliscom.blogspot.com/2007/02/spotlight-on-mom-Susannahh-wesley.html. Reprinted by permission.

5. Eliza Clarke, *Susannah Wesley* (London: W. H. Allen & Co., 1886), 68.

6. Just How Badly Do You Want It?

1. Summarization of "The Visitor," a drama written by John Alexander, from DramaShare.org, © 1998. Used by permission.

2. Lotz, *Just Give Me Jesus*, 63-64.

7. Getting Started

1. Lotz, *Just Give Me Jesus*, 95.

2. Copied by Stephen Ross for www.wholesomewords.org from *The Advanced Guard of Missions* by Clifford G. Howell. (Mountain View, Calif: Pacific Press Publishing, 1912). Used by permission.

9. Getting to Know Your God

1. Oswald Chambers, *My Utmost*, August 28.

2. Kay Arthur, *Lord, I Want to Know You* (Portland, Ore.: Multnomah, 1992), p. 13. Reprinted with permission from Precept Ministries International.

10. God's Love Letter to You

1. Reprinted with permission. *The New Strong's Exhaustive Concordance of the Bible*, James Strong, © 1990, Thomas Nelson, Inc. Nashville, Tenn. All rights reserved. Page 3; accompanying definition found in Greek Dictionary, p. 47.

2. Kay Arthur, *Lord, Teach Me to Pray in 28 Days* (Chattanooga: Precept Ministries International, 1982), 16. Reprinted with permission.

11. In Search of Your "Want-To"

1. Richard J. Foster, *Prayer: Finding the Heart's True Home* (San Francisco: HarperCollins Publishers, © 1992), 13. Reprinted with permission.

2. Tom Rogeberg, "Tim Tebow: Born to Lead," *Sharing the Victory* (Fellowship of Christian Athletes), August-September 2009, p. 10. Used by permission.

13. When God Is Silent

1. Reprinted by Permission. *Life Lessons with Max Lucado, Book of Acts*, Max Lucado, © 2006, Thomas Nelson, Inc. Nashville, Tenn. All rights reserved. Page vi.

2. *Trust His Heart*, Lyrics by Babbie Mason and Eddie Carswell, © 1989 May Sun Music (Admin. By Word Music, LLC), Word Music, LLC, Causing Change Music (Admin. By Dayspring Music, LLC), Dayspring Music, LLC), Dayspring Music, LLC. All Rights Reserved. Used By Permission.

3. Stephen Curtis Chapman, *Sometimes He Comes in the Clouds*, © 1995 Sparrow Song (BMI) (adm. By EMI CMG Publishing)/ Peach Hill Songs (MBI) All rights reserved. Used by permission.

14. Prayerlessness

1. Lotz, *Just Give Me Jesus*, 230-35.
2. Ibid., 234.
3. Ibid., 234-35.

15. The Power of Prayer

1. Extracted from *D. L. Moody: Moody Without Sankey*, by John Pollock, in the Foreward by Luis Palau (Scotland, UK: Christian Focus Publications, www.christianfocus.com, © 1995). Used with permission.
2. Dr. R. A. Torrey, *Why God Used D. L. Moody*, a sermon, 1923. Copyright held by Sword of the Lord Publishers, Murfreesboro, Tenn. Used by permission.
3. Chambers, *My Utmost*, August 28.

16. Final Confessions from My Slacker's Heart

1. Chambers, *My Utmost*, May 12.
2. Quote from *Pray Continuously*, sermon by Pastor Pete Wilson, Cross Point Community Church, Nashville, Tenn.; March 29, 2009.
3. Reprinted by permission. *Peace, A Fruit of the Spirit Study Guide*, Calvin Miller, © 2008, Thomas Nelson, Inc., Nashville, Tenn. All rights reserved. Page 38.